Tuesdays, Heartbreaks, and Soulmates

Tuesdays,
Heartbreaks,
and Soulmates

JULIE CRAWFORD

author & photographer

Jaden and Trinity. You are my break in the clouds, my light in the darkness, and my greatest reason for choosing to wake up and show up in this life, for creating myself, for healing. Thank you for allowing the opportunity to experience the one role I have dreamed of being since I was a little girl, Mom. May you both soar throughout your lives bravely spreading your unique truths and embracing your most authentic and unapologetic selves. I am so proud of you both for all you are and will become in this lifetime.

Anthony, my brother and my friend. You are my saving grace. I do not know if I will ever compose a set of words precious enough to describe how much you mean to me. Until then, here are some lyrics to suffice: "May we sit together when we're grey and old, on cloud nine." - *Ben Howard*

Mom and Dad. You are my foundation in life. Thank you for the unconditional love and continuous support you have given me, even when I did not make it easy. Thank you both for teaching me the value of family, quality time, and the wonders life has to offer.

John Mayer, a stranger in this lifetime, but quite possibly a dear connection from a past life. I have built homes within your songs. Your energy resonates in a way that makes me feel like everything will be okay and creates a safe place for me to rest, realign, and thrive again. Holding on to your music gives me a sense of peace like nothing else in the world has yet to be able to do. Thank you for riding shotgun on road trips, harmonizing with the sounds of nature on all my adventures, and for that unforgettable Tuesday in Nashville when my vital signs jumped from my body to yours.

Lesley, Amy, Rachel, Kandi, and Shannon. You are soul sisters near and dear to my heart. Thank you for the space you hold for me to show up in the world just as I am and for allowing me to learn the true meaning of friendship. May you always remember how deeply I cherish our loving connection and the time we share.

Eight years, I have lived an empowering and adventurous journey, navigating the depths of my soul, to ~~find~~ create the absolute favorite version of my authentic self. The path has not been an easy one by any means, but it has been the most rewarding experience beyond anything I had ever imagined it to be, guiding me to a life I am proud to call mine.

The foundation of the fulfilling life I live today was built through my family long ago. Growing up we went on adventures out west, snow skiing and RV trips exploring National Parks across the country, spending quality time together, and choosing connection. I was raised a witness to two people who choose each other day after day, as life partners, carrying the most beautiful love ever known. Deep down I wanted all of those same elements in my own life, but somewhere along the way I got lost without knowing I was. Looking back I could blame it on a number things—social conditioning, a broken religion, past life trauma, bad choices—but ultimately, fear was the root of all.

One of the most frightening obstacles I had to overcome was the fear of rejection causing me to be unwilling to speak from the heart. Truth be told, I let the fear control my thoughts so much that I never even took the time to get to know who I wanted to be without the opinion of others. I would shape myself to form the person I thought someone wanted me to be in order to gain acceptance, even if that sacrifice hindered true fulfillment.

For years, I remained disconnected from myself, repeating the same lessons with different people, failing to learn that I was keeping myself stuck in a wounded pattern. When I started becoming conscious of the fact that I had been living a life not of my own, I did not want to be seen as a failure in another's eyes. I kept my burdens tucked away, until they could no longer be contained. Call it a knowing through the blood bond we share, in a serendipitous moment, my brother sent me a song titled

"Break In The Clouds" and my walls began to crack. Always family but never friends, music broke the barrier and opened the doors to a friendship I never dreamed possible, one built on the foundation of unconditional love. Through songs, feeling truly seen, I began gaining a sense of who I wanted to be and the versions that needed to be left behind.

In February of 2014, a singer-songwriter performed an acoustic set in my living room. This was the first time we met. Whatever resonating energy transferred from his body and into mine when we hugged goodbye that night fueled my inner flame, setting ablaze my passionate search for everything. Just weeks after this undeniably fated interaction with a kindred spirit, I found myself amidst an experience that would forever change the course of my life. On a mountaintop in Alaska with my dad, not another person in sight, he tells me that he feels closer to God standing in the presence of those majestic mountains than sitting on any pew. His words struck a chord within, and I felt exalted. I knew, then and there, the type of love and connection I was seeking in everyone else had to start from within. Getting re-connected with adventure would be the key to self-discovery. With the northern lights as witness, I made a promise to myself that I would be brave enough to step into my divine power and seek my truth no matter the distance I would have to travel to find the way to myself. And so, the journey began.

Fall that year, in October, I met a tender and loving man who would become a muse. Through his eyes, I was shown visions of the woman I wanted to be, and he held space for this self to grow. Although our transformational connection would dissipate within one year, the strive to become all he reflected never faded. I began traveling alone, including taking the almost month-long road trip that he and I talked about going on together. I unlocked a foreign love for solitude, something I never gave myself a change to experience. I poured out my emotions in diaries knowing that my most vulnerable thoughts could remain safely hidden in the pages, and I stumbled upon a love for poetry.

As self-love and *my* acceptance of my own were evolving and false layers shedding, I began sharing small facets of the prismatic woman awakening from within with people who held space for a piece or two of the divine puzzle. I call each of these kindred spirits a Soulmate. These amazing human beings colliding into mine along the way inspired a whole new expansion within my inner and outer world; some knowingly and others barely remembering our crossing of paths. There are even a handful of people who have no clue that I exist, and the energy they put out into the world, through their creative arts, has fabricated homes in my heart. Indeed, I believe strangers can be soulmates too. By my definition, they are people who reflect pieces of our soul's truth that only they have the power mirror, or at least the ability to show it in a way that we can recognize. Regardless of the fated outcome, I carry the people and memories with me, and I always will. They are a part of me, each a chapter in the story of becoming my very favorite version of self.

In this book, I share fragments of time that have weaved themselves into the celestial fibers of my existence. As a reader, you will find letters of past and present connections—people, places, and memories that I turned into poetry. Pages are filled with self-reflection discovered in lyrical verses and Mother Nature's churches. There are photographs from solo adventures where I pushed beyond my comfort zone in order to expand and learn who I was when no one else was around. Most profoundly, there are moments where I found the strength to let myself be seen by the people I love the most.

- Julie

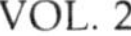

VOL. 2

the kind of love that
brings you home

Tuesdays, Heartbreaks, and Soulmates

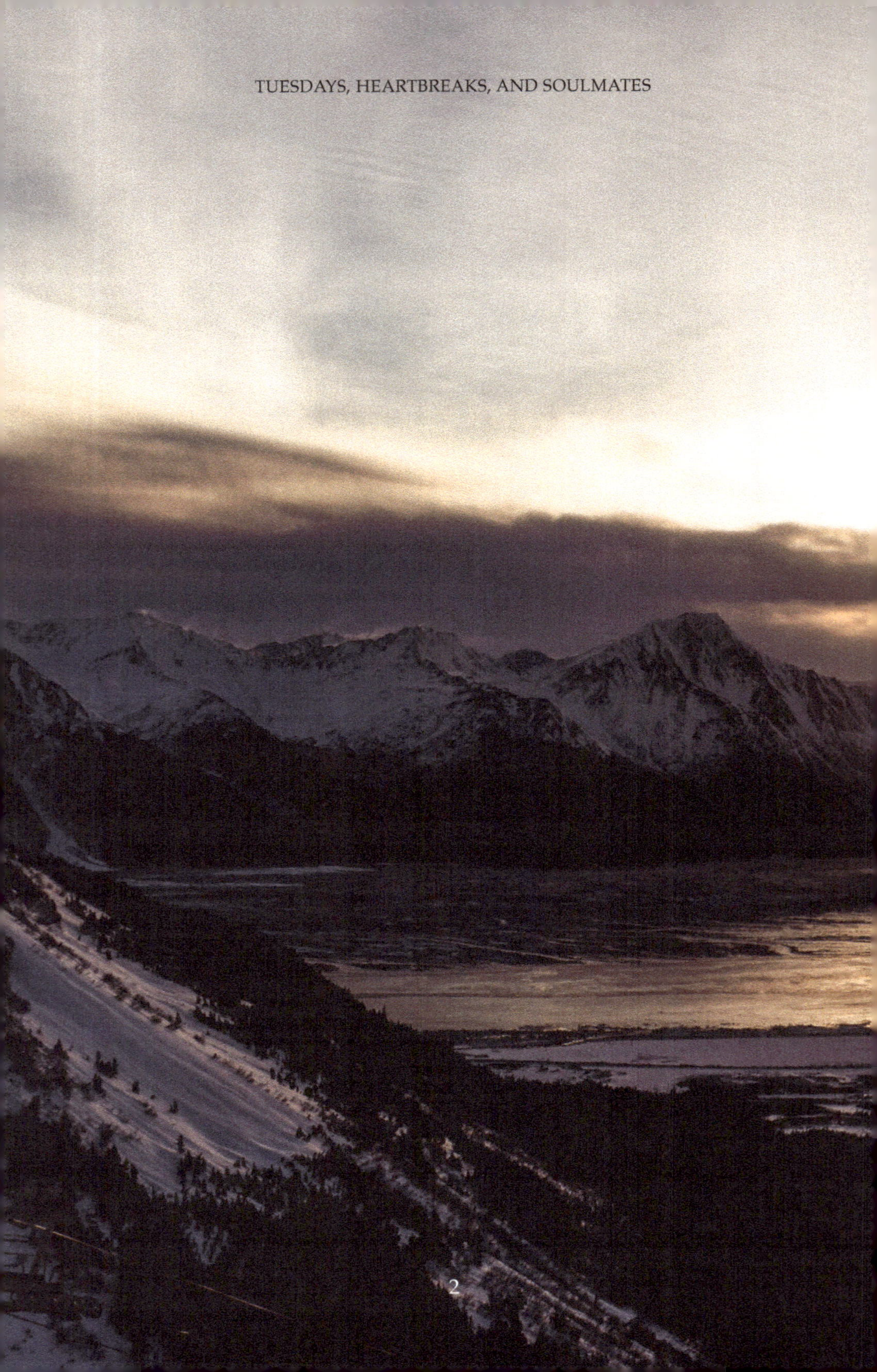

religion of nature

I have found pieces of me
buried in adventure
inner-light, truth, and
ultimately, self-love
all because sacred lands
hold space for us to exist
as our most authentic selves

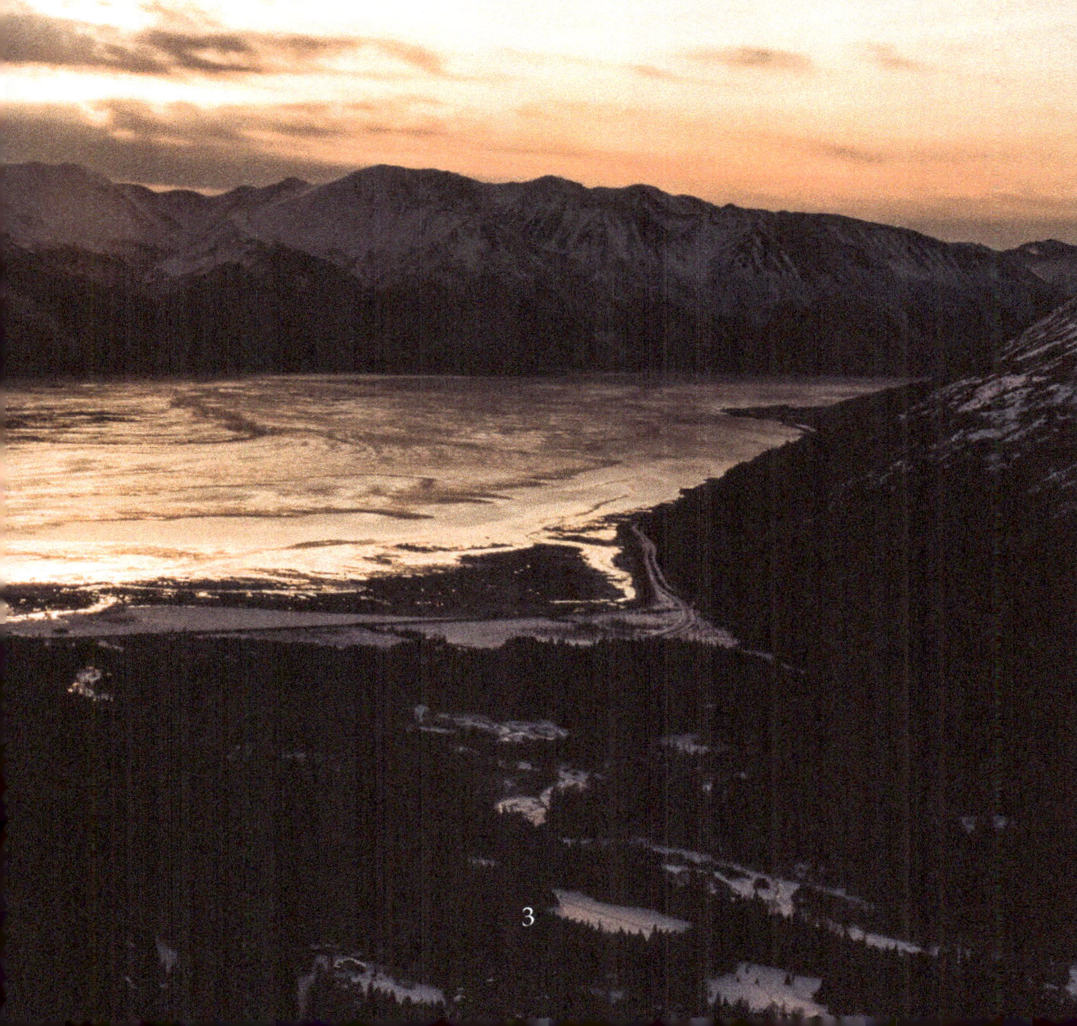

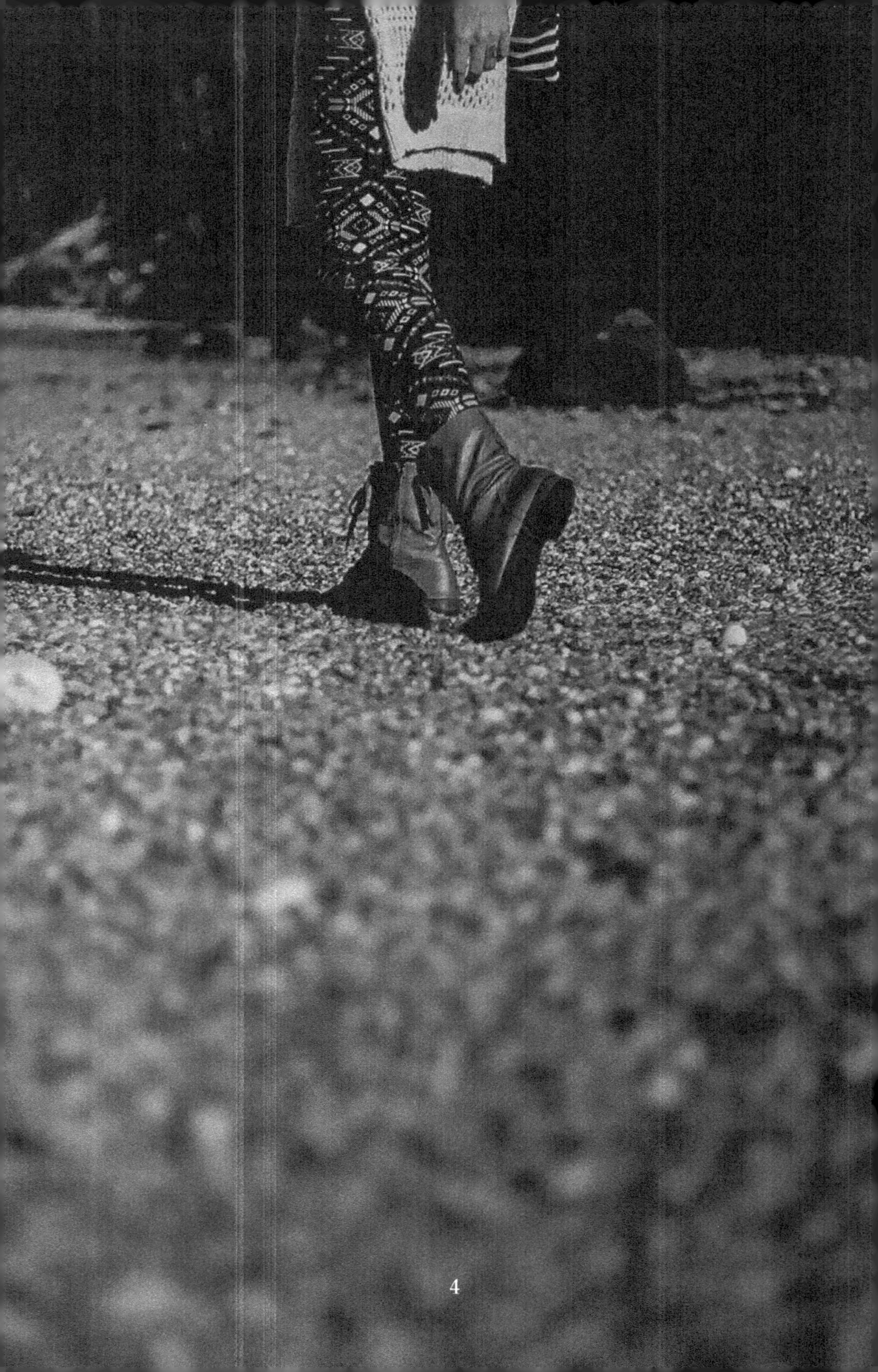

There she stood

a lost poet with a broken heart

Sunlight beaming down

burdens eclipse the inked pages

Then she remembers the light

that *illuminates* within

Mustering courage to walk alone

Burning versions of a past self

that hold her back from destiny

She walks through the shadows

to find the poetry

Find home

One, two, three, four

I declare *delicate* thumb war

Tracing constellations on her skin

Star trails burn through the mind

Shaking frost off fragile hearts

Finding peace within the walls

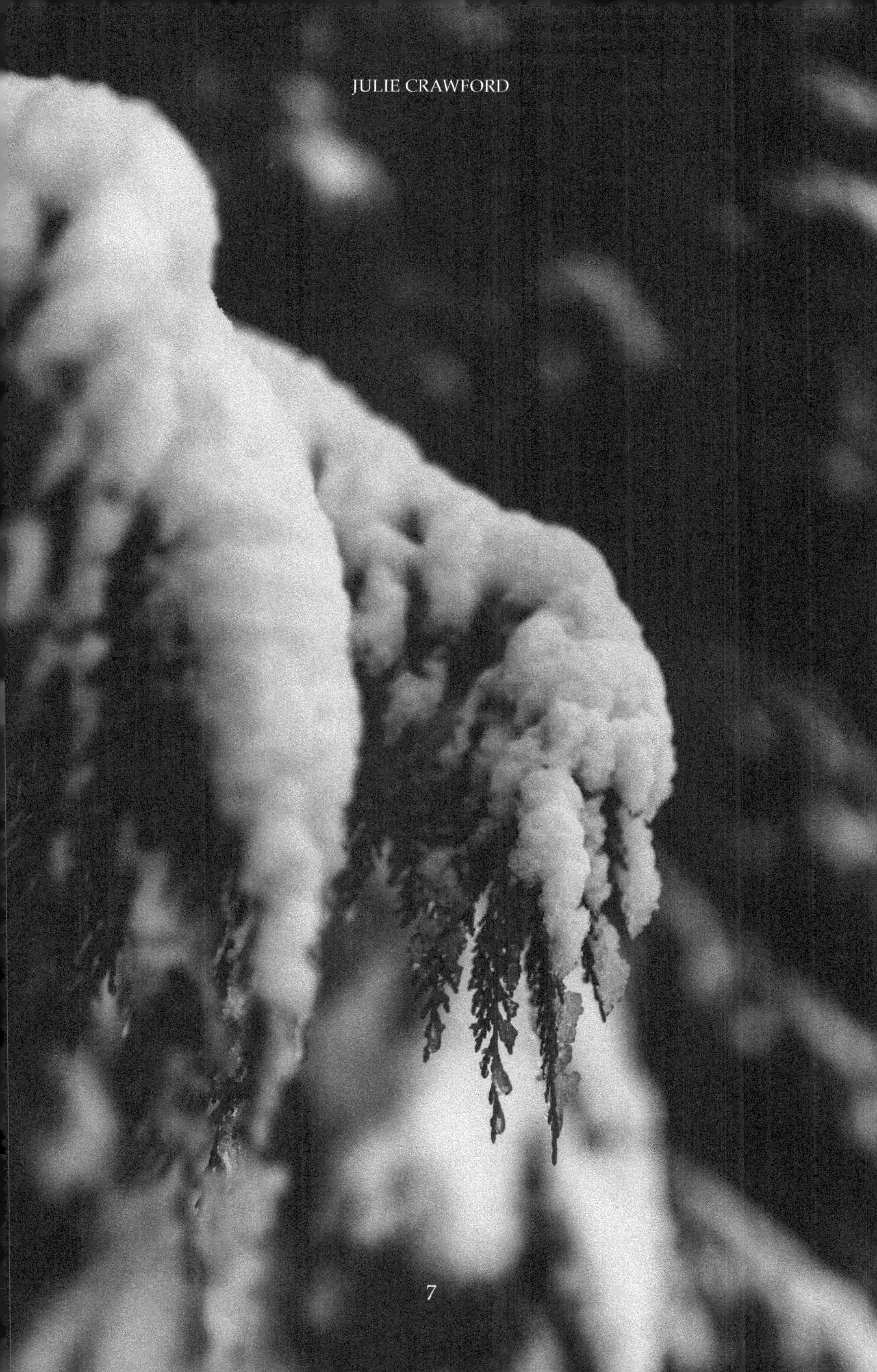
JULIE CRAWFORD

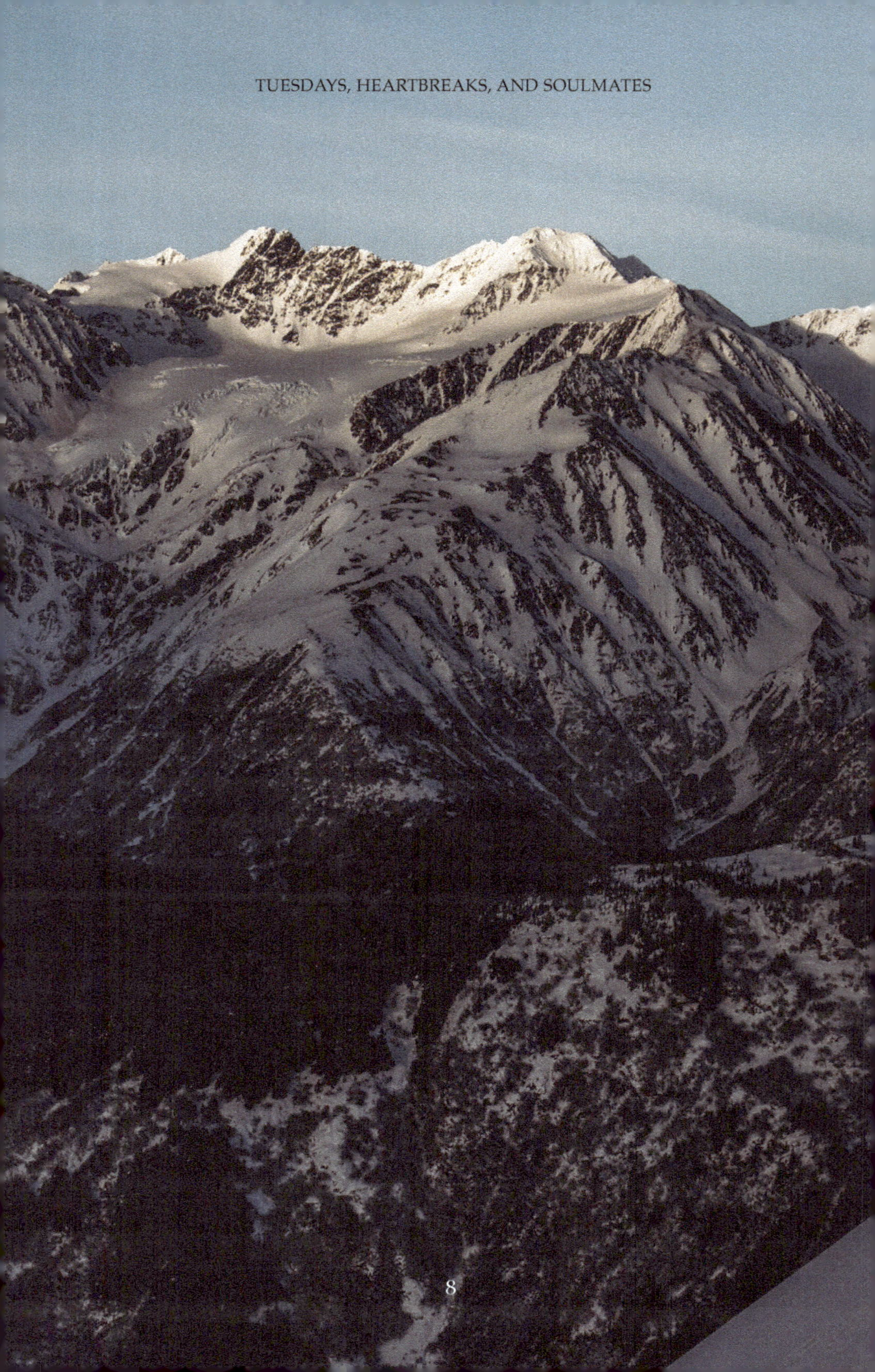

I write for you, for me,

for the *breaking* of all

barriers that separate us from

a life of wondrous fulfillment

Darkness lurked in my past
but you were never scared
to hold my hand in the shadows

You have always believed
in my strength deeply hidden
buried in lies I told myself
to defend the pain within

Finding how to open the doors
one heartfelt song at a time
music broke the barriers

You taught me how
family become friends
loving me when I could not
You are my *saving grace*

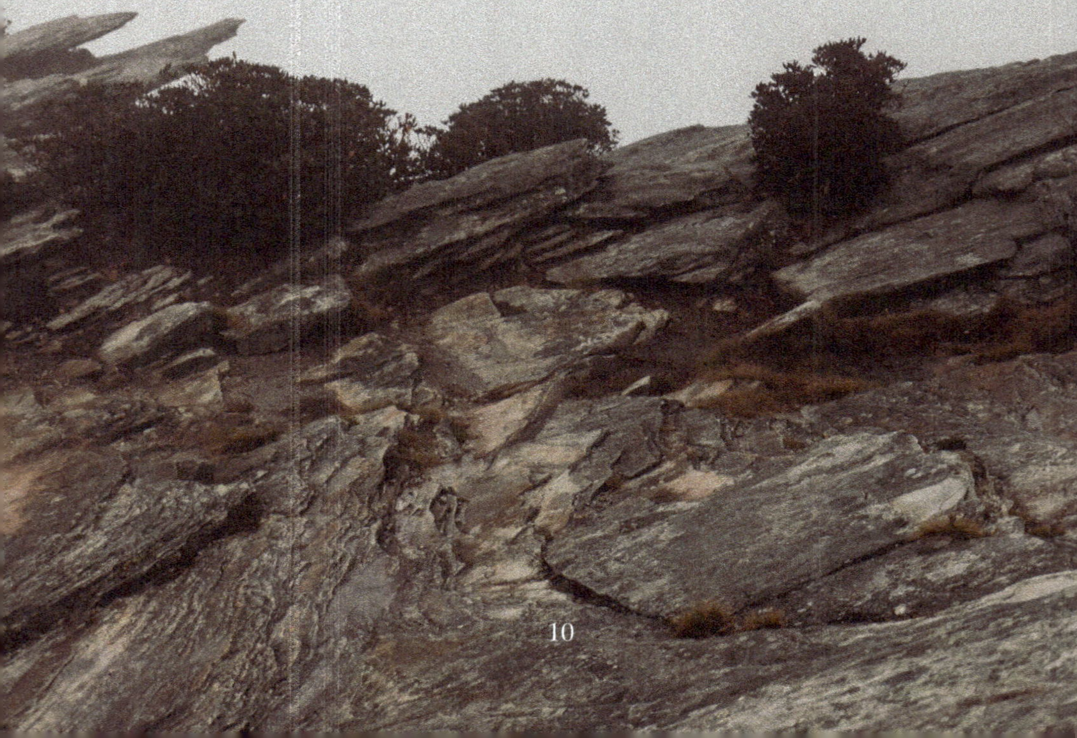

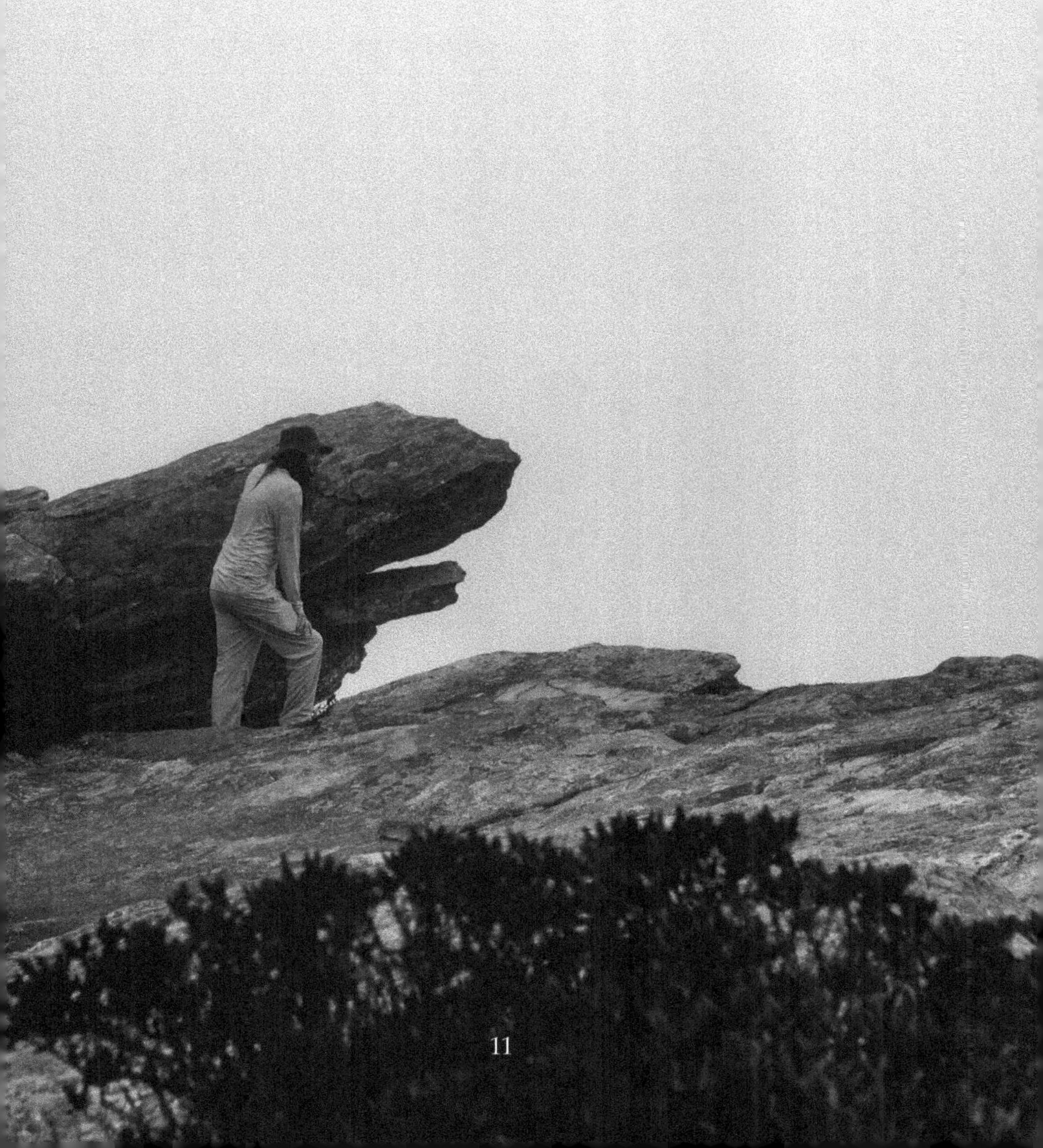

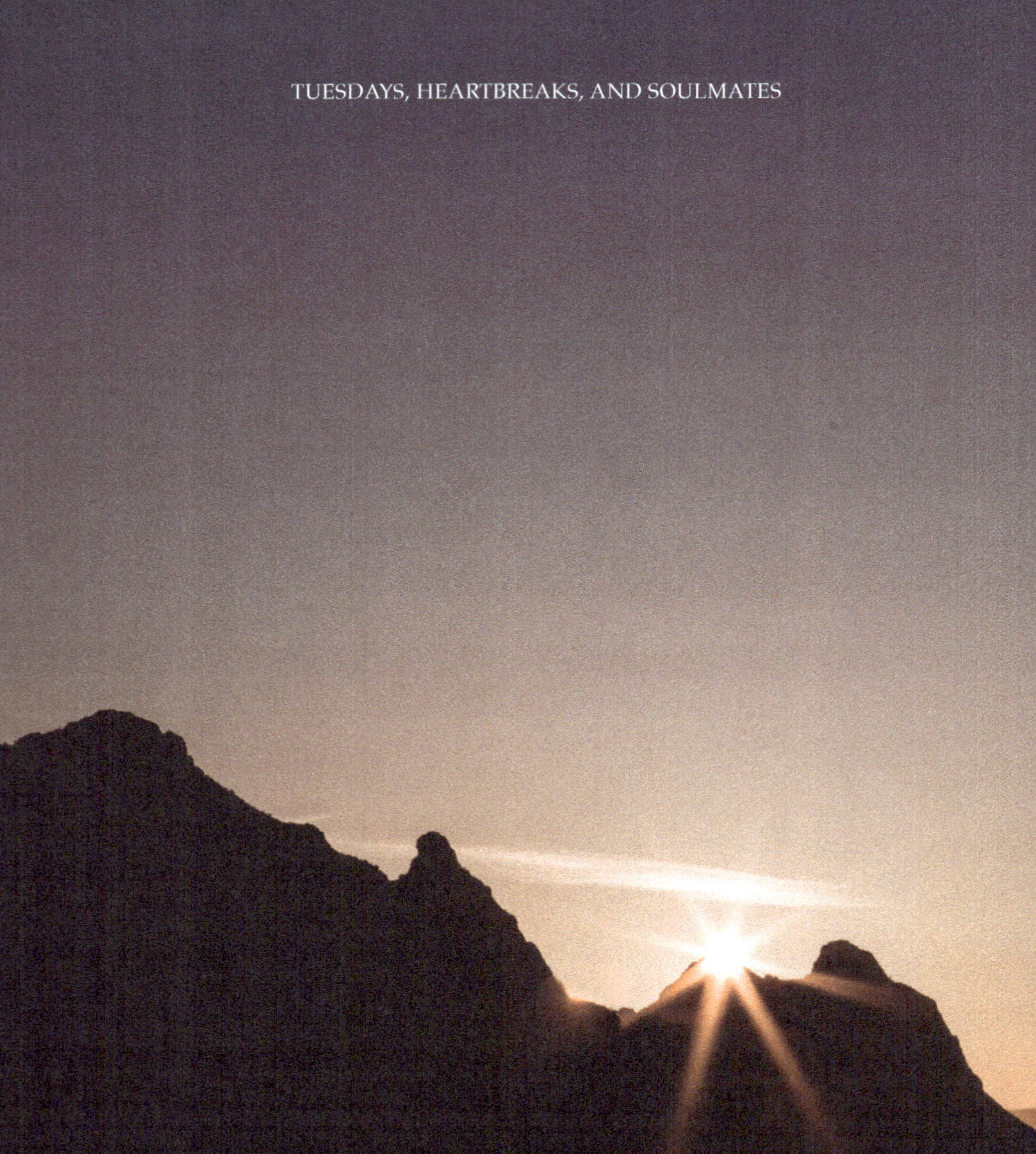

Wildest dreams are born here amidst ethereal spaces

Gleaming from the deepest parts of inward self

Serene presence in the awe-surrounding moments

Belonging to a *universe* greater than I know

Tapping into my personal power and enlightenment

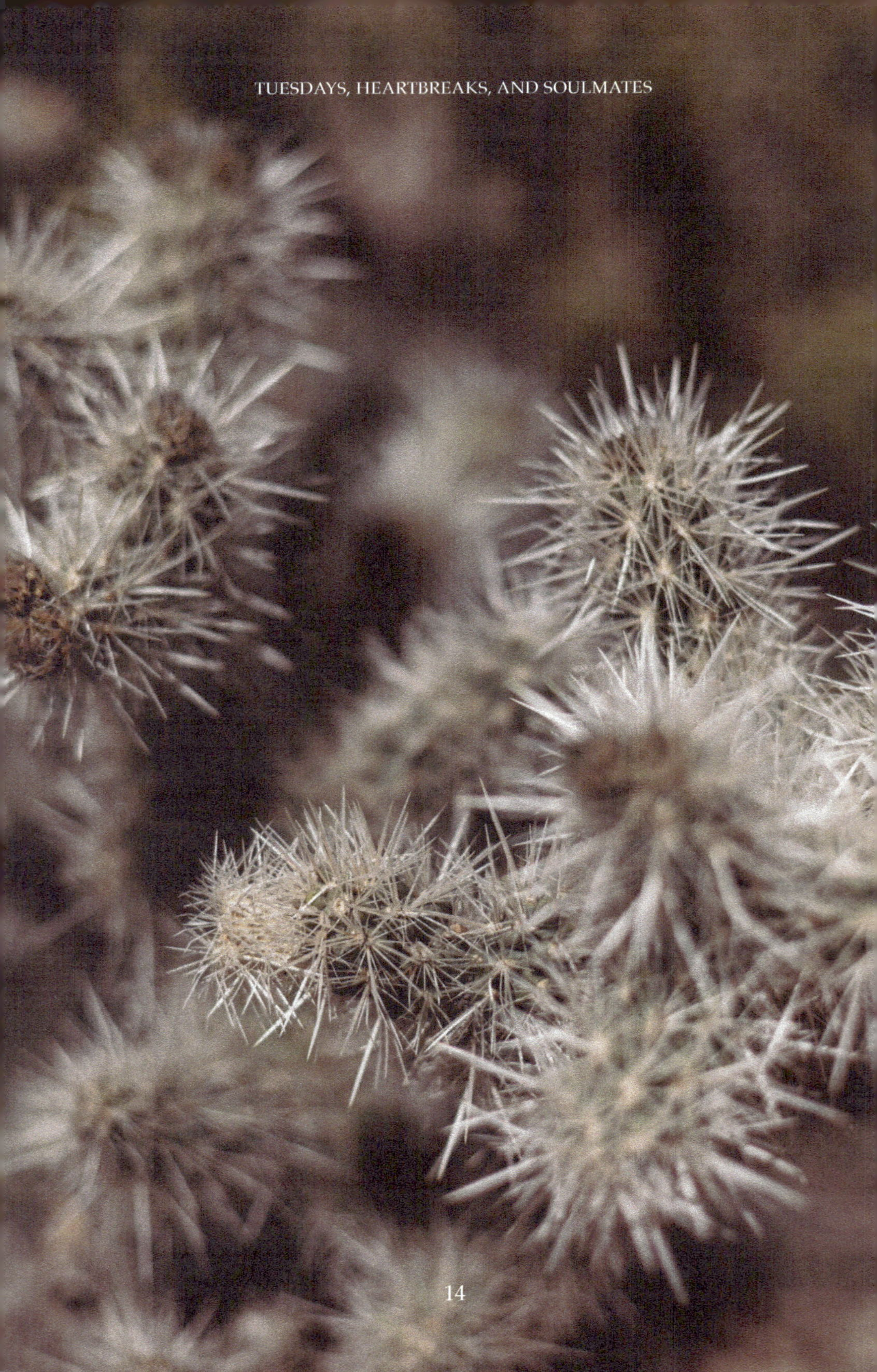

March 22, 2016

Dear Heart,

What the actual fuck are you doing?
Driving off on a Tuesday, leaving every bit of comfort behind.
All you have is your dad's old tent, camera, and the essentials.
You do not even know where you are going to sleep tonight,
much less what is to come on this journey *(aka spiritual quest).*
There are wolves out there in the darkness, you know.
Remember how cactus needles trigger childhood trauma?
You are going to step on one in the middle of the desert and
a kind stranger will help but quickly lose compassion after
the second time because he thinks you are absolutely insane.
Maybe you are, after all, thinking you can do this trip alone.
Do you really believe you are actually going to follow through
with secretly jumping out of the plane in your favorite place?
There is a campground with a $2 shower and a black widow.
You will have a real panic attack with shampoo in your hair.
Probably safer to quit now and save yourself the painful mess.

Sincerely,
Fear

25 days and 7027 miles later...

Dear Heart,

You did it, proving psychological limits wrong.
Courageously completing a life-changing adventure,
with music and nature to keep you company.
Setting the tone for confidence and perseverance.

Sincerely,
Expanding *Mind*

Whispers of *nostalgia*

a sense of belonging

Intuition speaks softly

a spiritual déjà vu

Desire for heartfelt connection

a bond to something real

Integrated into my existence

the immeasurable value of family

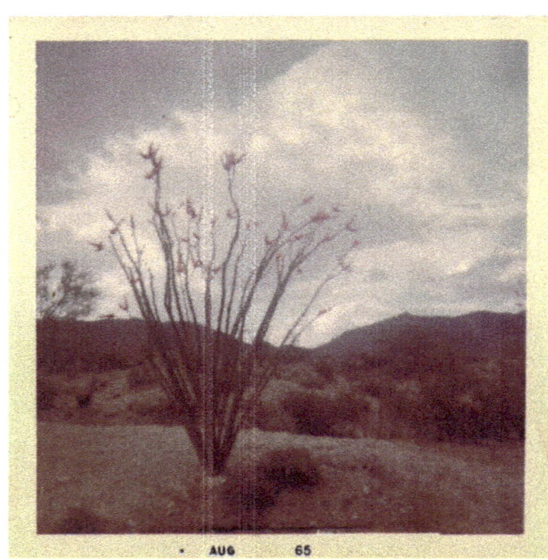

Photo taken by my grandmother in the area where my dad was raised. I found the vintage print with her writing on the back five years after I, unknowingly, took a very similiar frame—a gentle reminder from the other side of life that this path I am on, crafted in love & adventure, is divine fate.

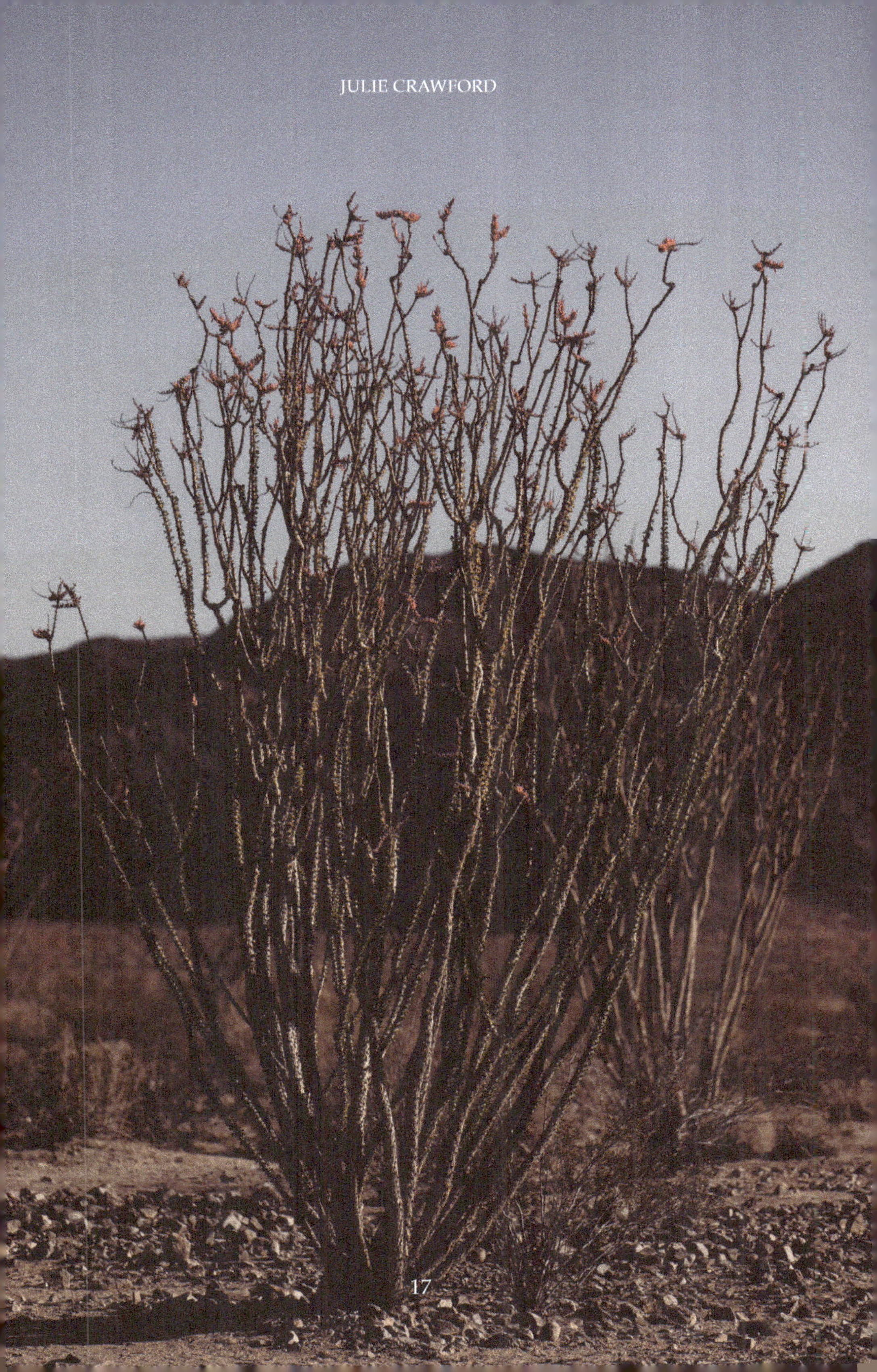

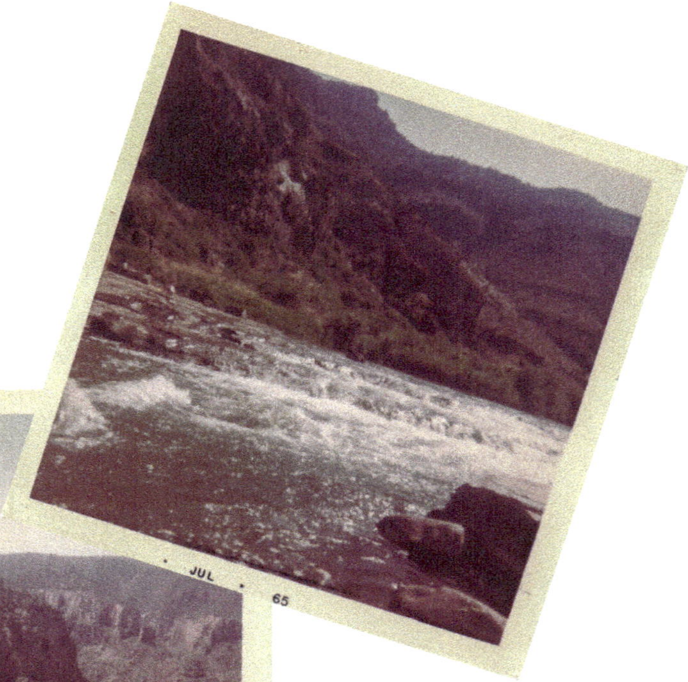

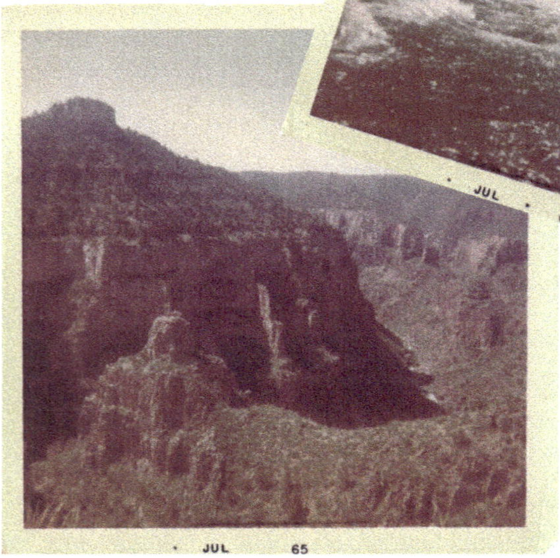

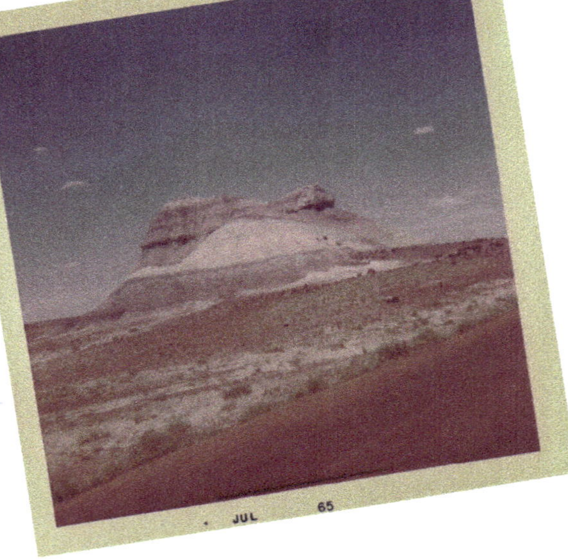

Salt River Canyon
July 4, 1965

Painted Desert
July 4, 1964

Old Faithful
Yellowstone Nat. Park
Sept, 1965

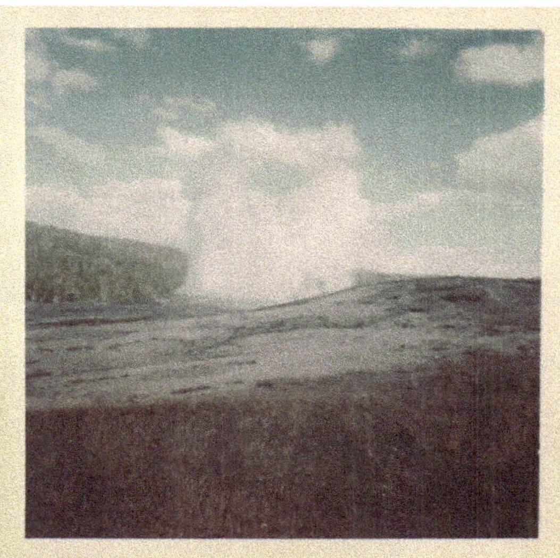

Nebraska
Sept 1965

Rocky Mtns
Sept 1965

Durango Colorado
Sept 1965

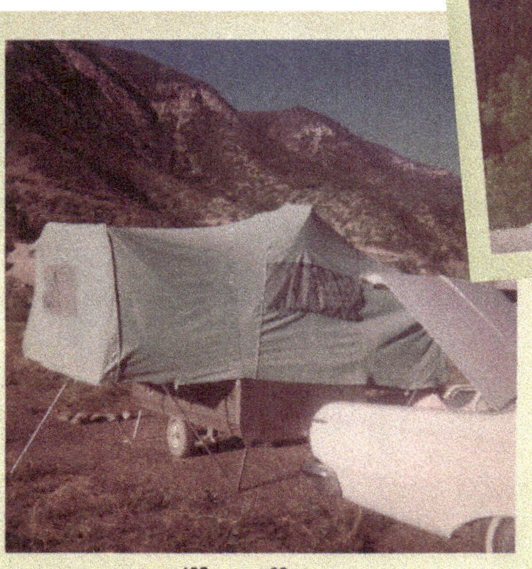

Thirst for the past

where we did not hide

pieces from one another

no secrets, no lies

a *peaceful* easy feeling

Missing her deeply

the wholesome woman

that felt like home

lost in the madness

of desert *wildfires*

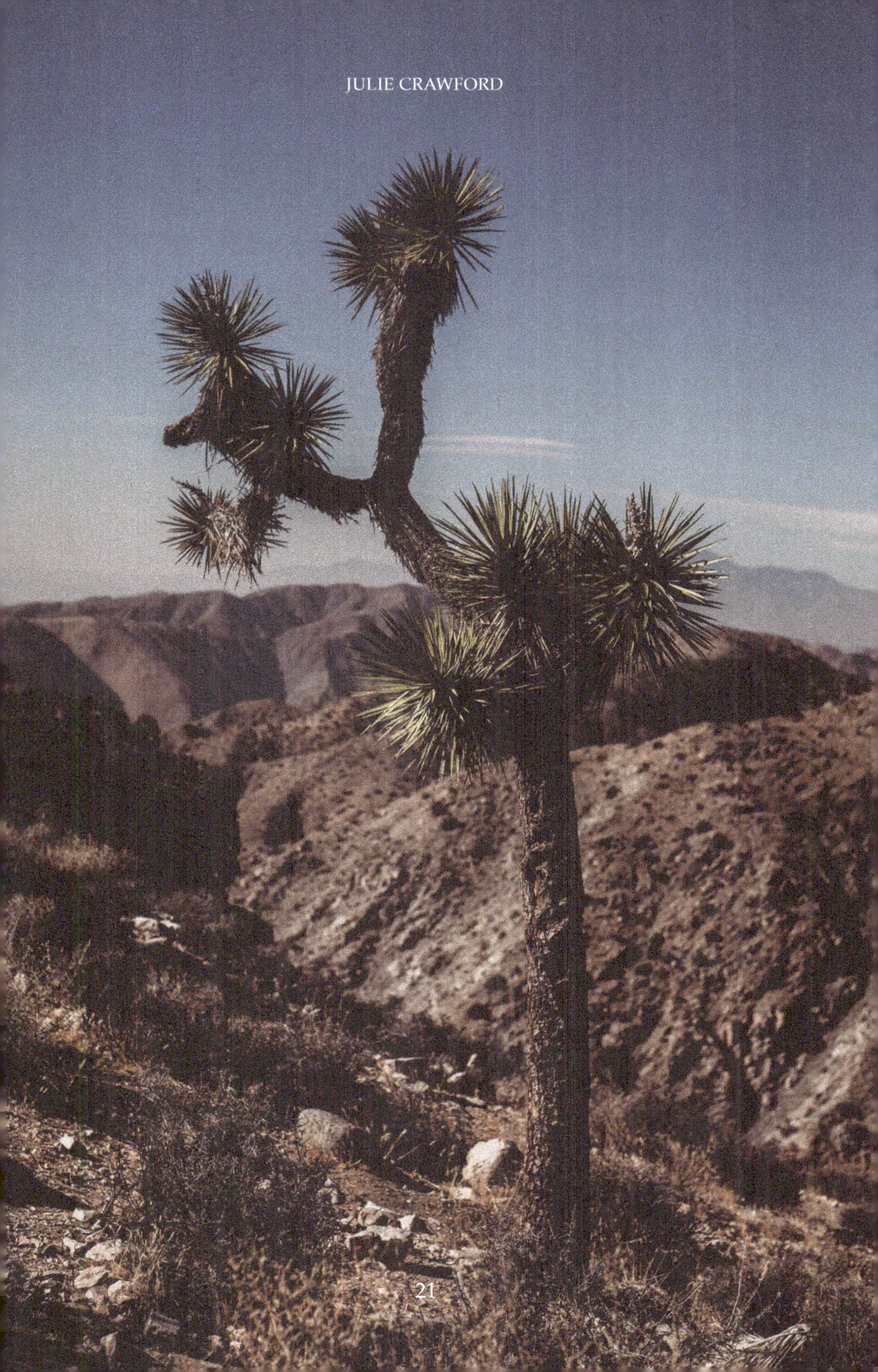

Easter morning

alone in the desert

sun rising over the hills

my very own Sunrise Service

unlike any that came before

those told to be fulfilling

but never actually were

Adventure is wholehearted

graceful and honest

holy and powerful

In the depths of my soul

amidst the wild, I found God

the self-manifestation in

Mother Nature's *churches*

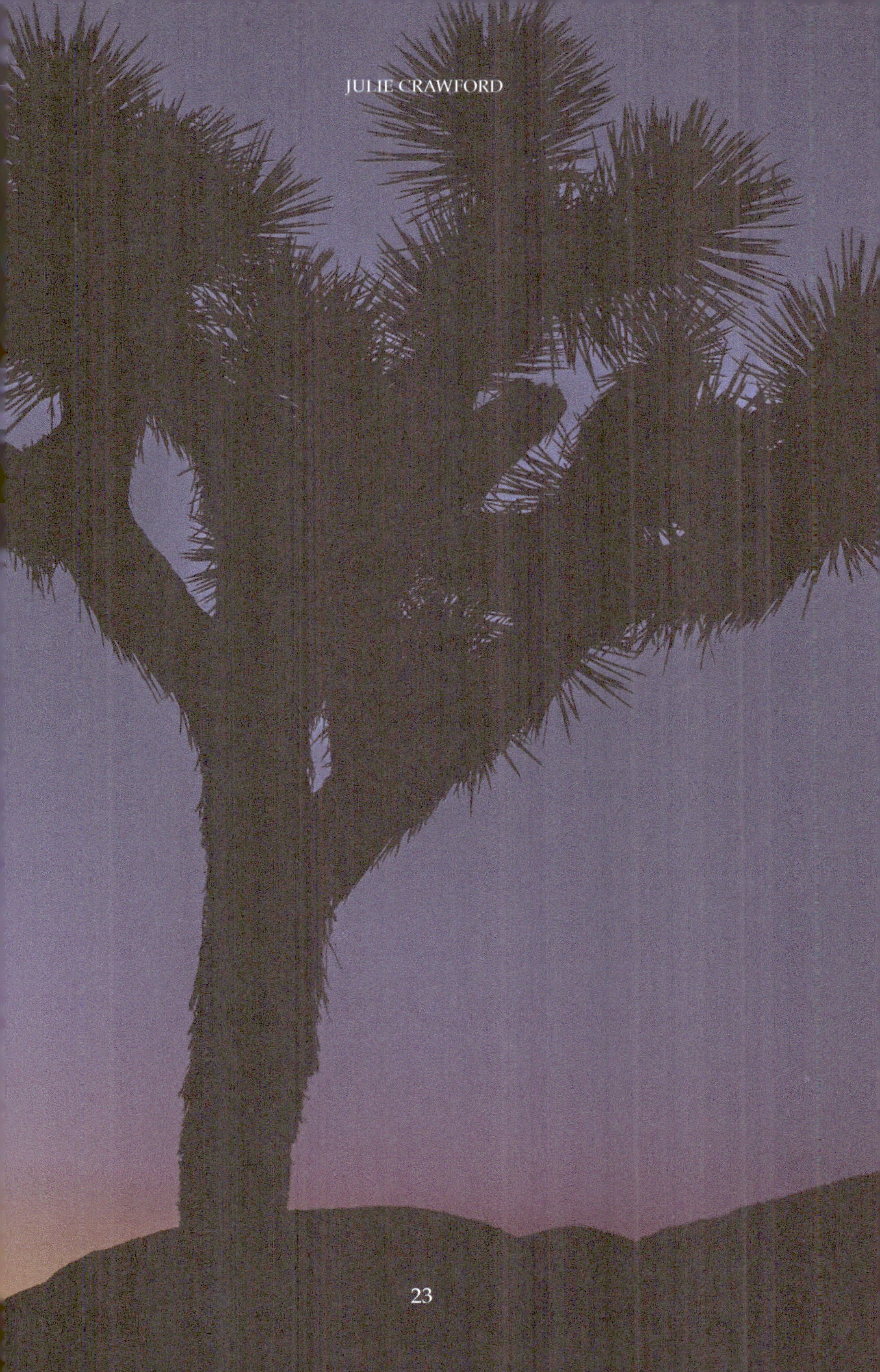

Lyrics you gave to me

held the keys to unlock

the *dazzling* soul

lost inside a dark dungeon

through the shadows

You were my guiding light

leading me back home

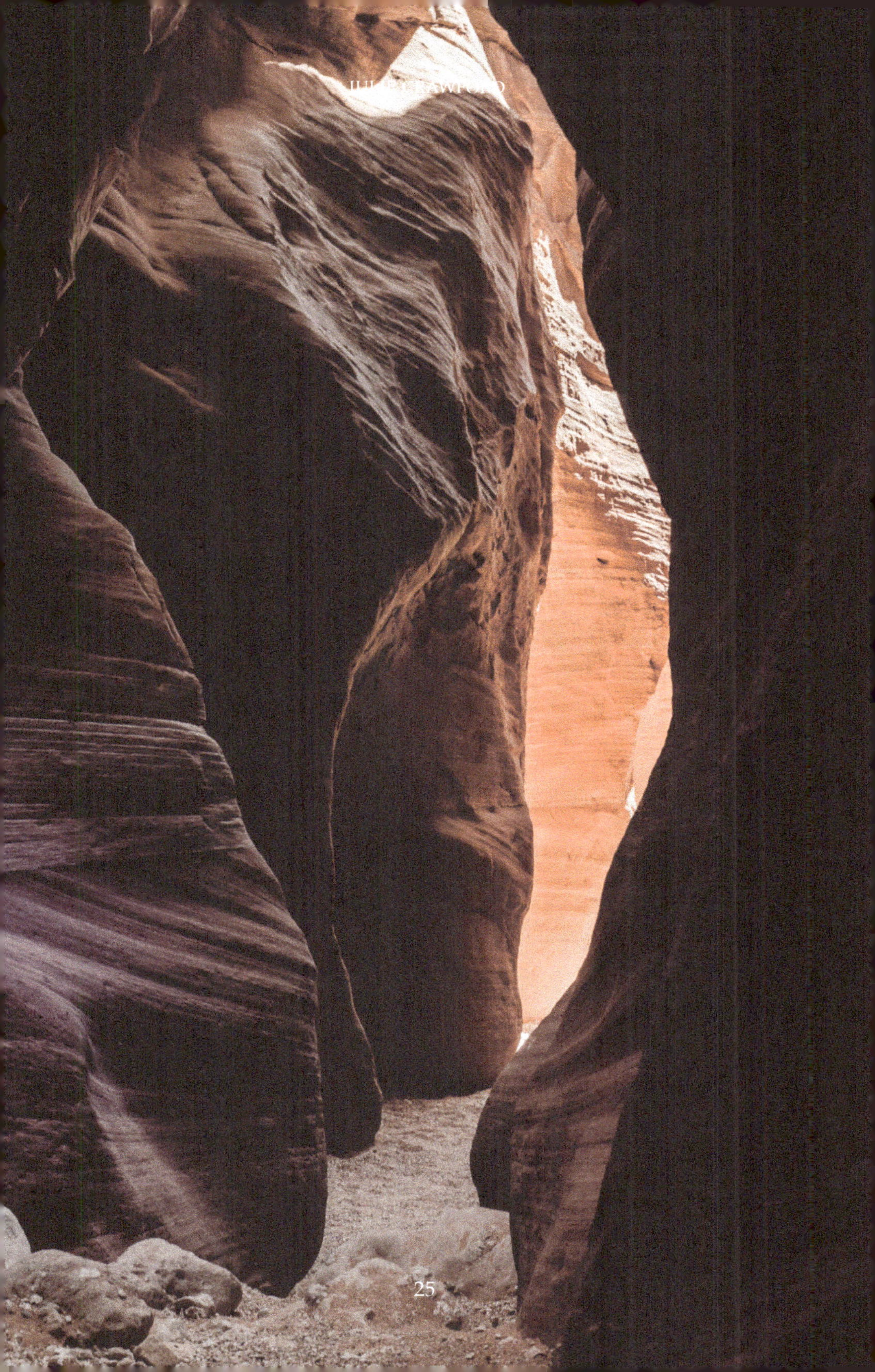

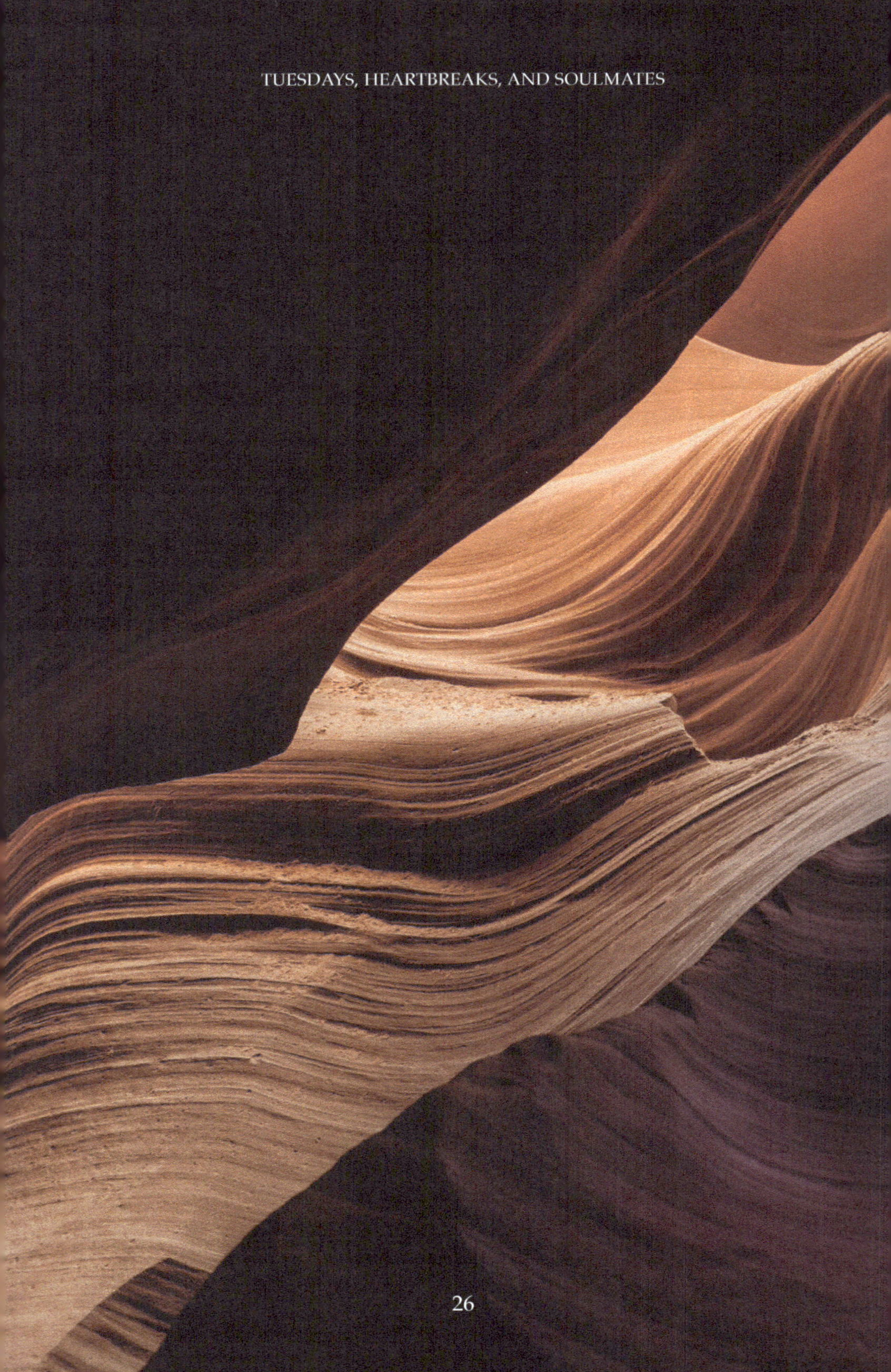

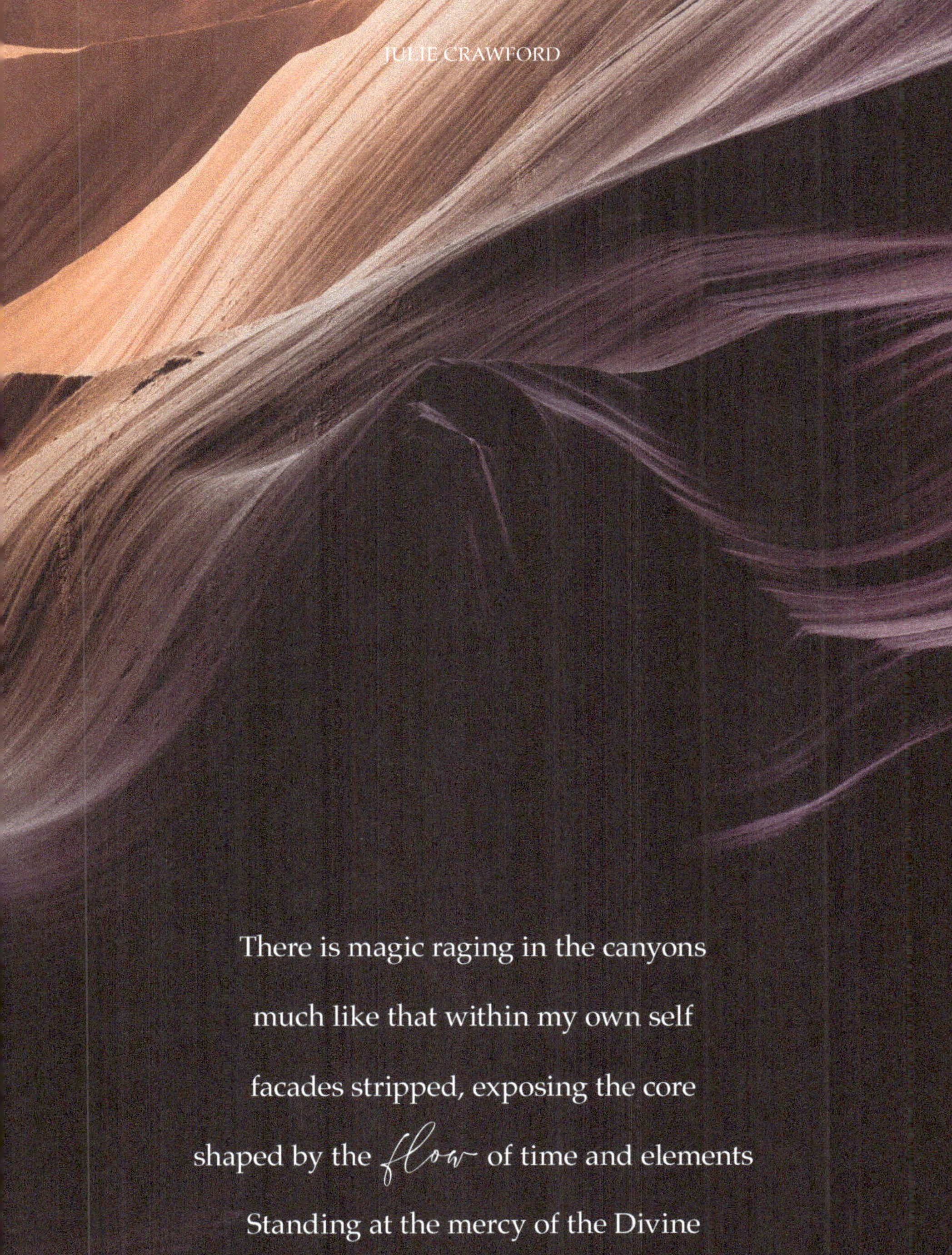

There is magic raging in the canyons

much like that within my own self

facades stripped, exposing the core

shaped by the *flow* of time and elements

Standing at the mercy of the Divine

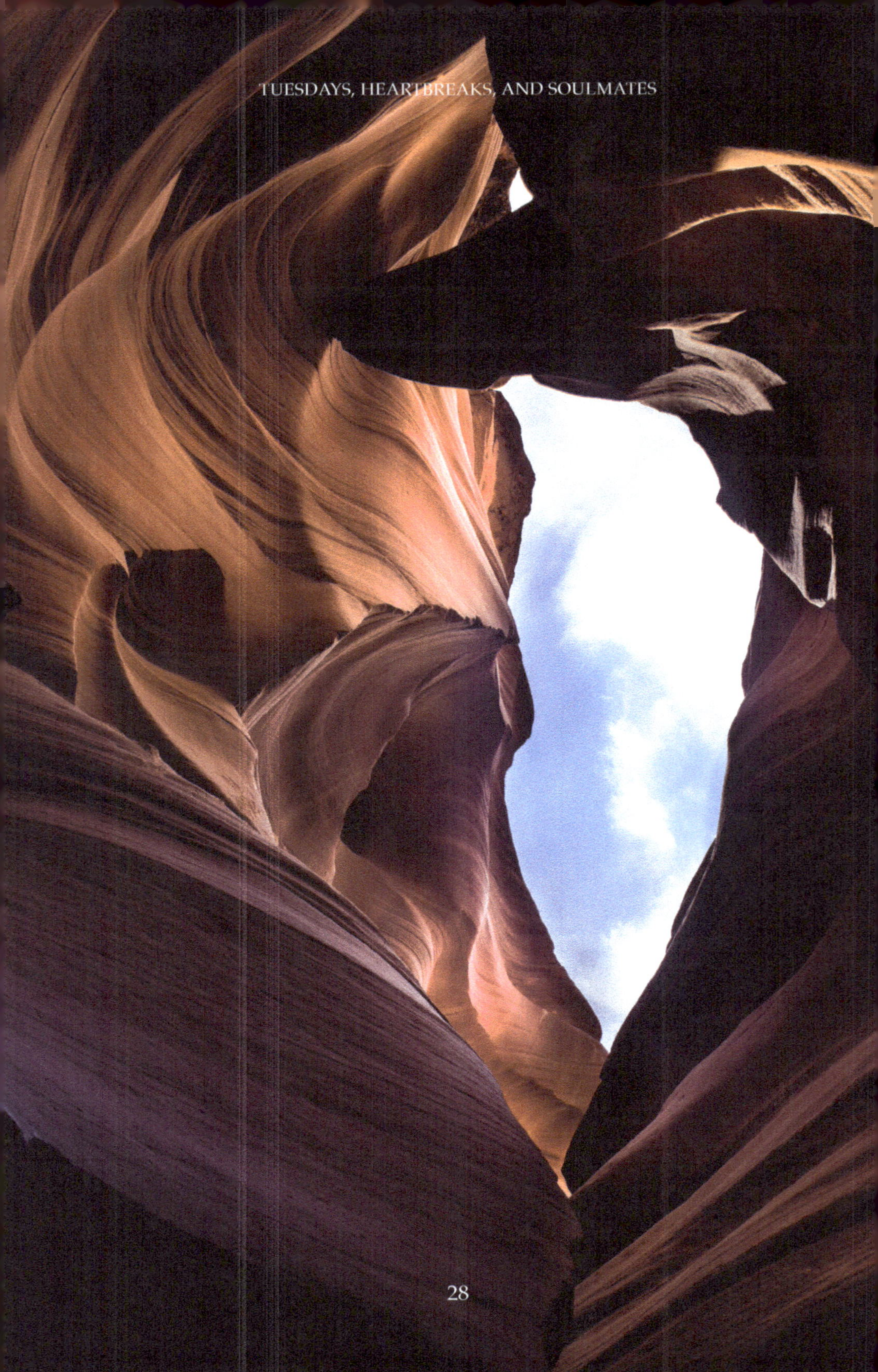

Standing in awe
gazing up at the bright sky
peeking through the canyon
I think to myself
This is so *surreal*

How does something so extraordinary exist
much less be standing in the depths of it?

Powerful trembles soar through my body
encased in the marvelous creation
I feel a connection to everything around me
almost as if the spirits of the jagged canyons
are speaking directly to me

Voices of my own consciousness
screaming from within
buried behind walls just waiting to be molded
shaped into something as incredibly unique
as these sandstones hidden in the cracks

My *light* is about to surface

She takes a deep breath

Lungs expanding

Hair blows wildly in the wind

Forces of rage crash down

Chilling splashes as the water

Collides into rocks

Falling back into herself

Goosebumps cover her body

Chills from *the mist*

She stretches her arms high

Heart expanding

Goosebumps cover her body

Chills from *the metaphor*

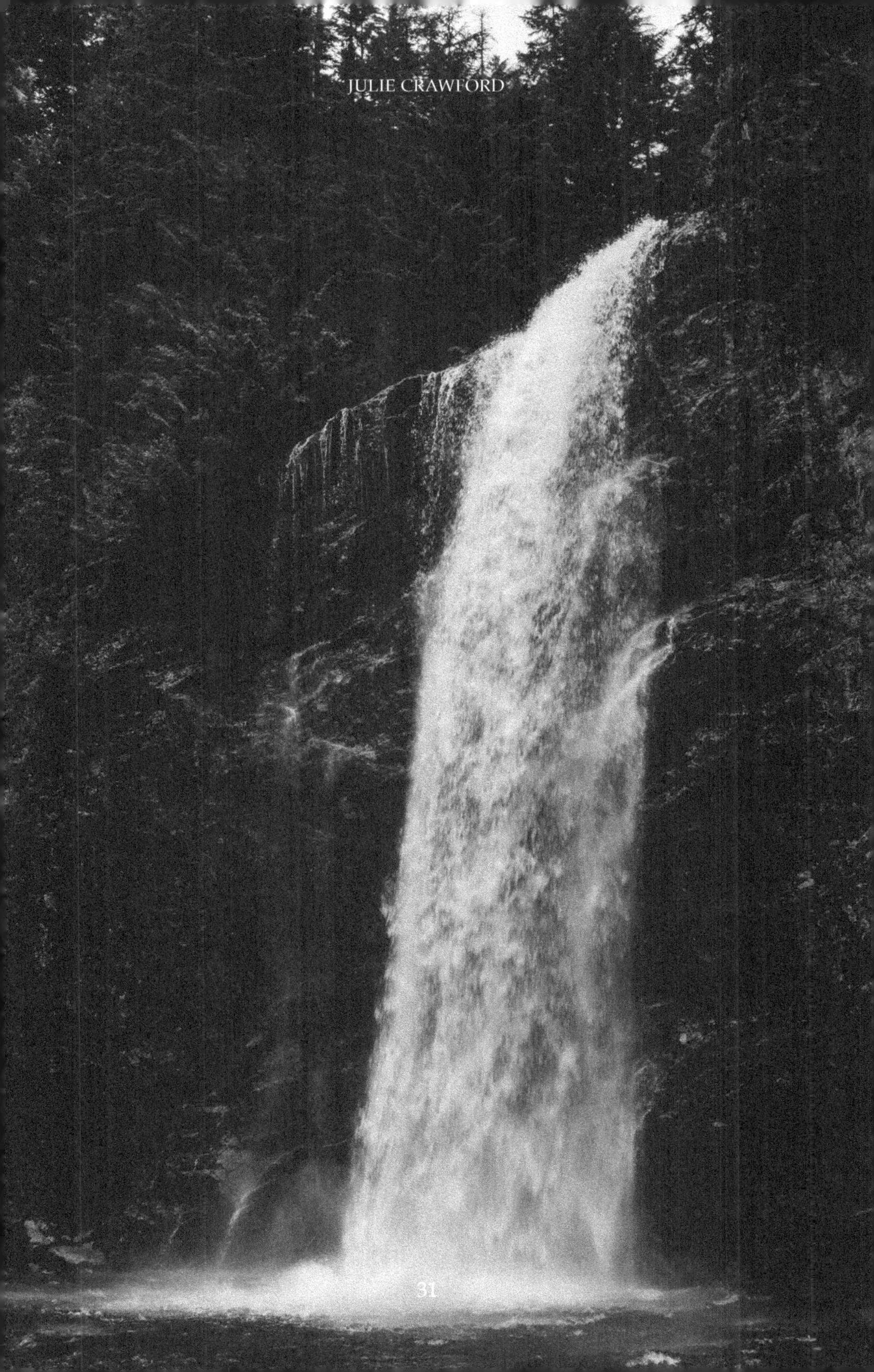
JULIE CRAWFORD
JULIE CRAWFORD

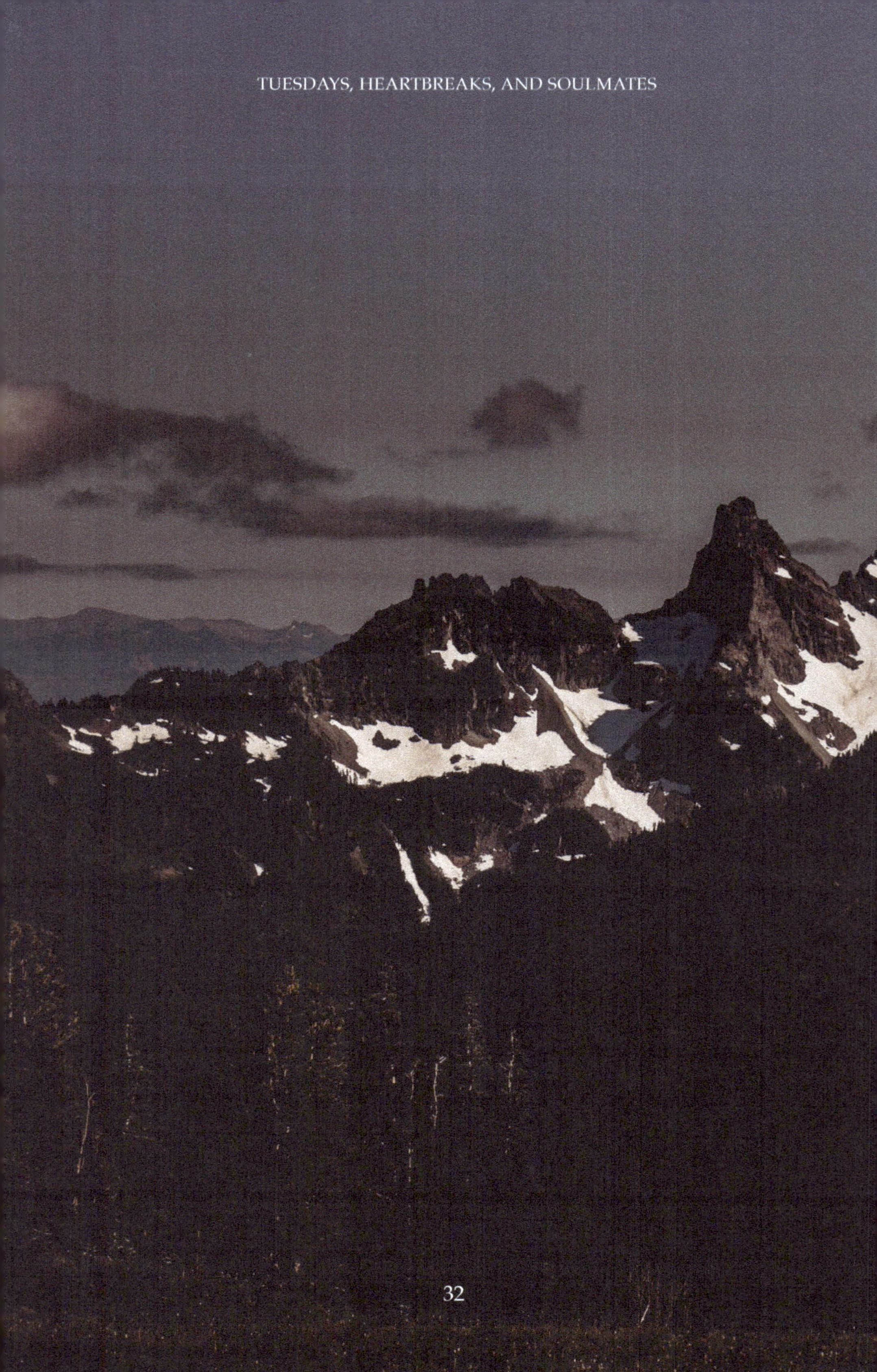

fear ceases to exist in your *presence*

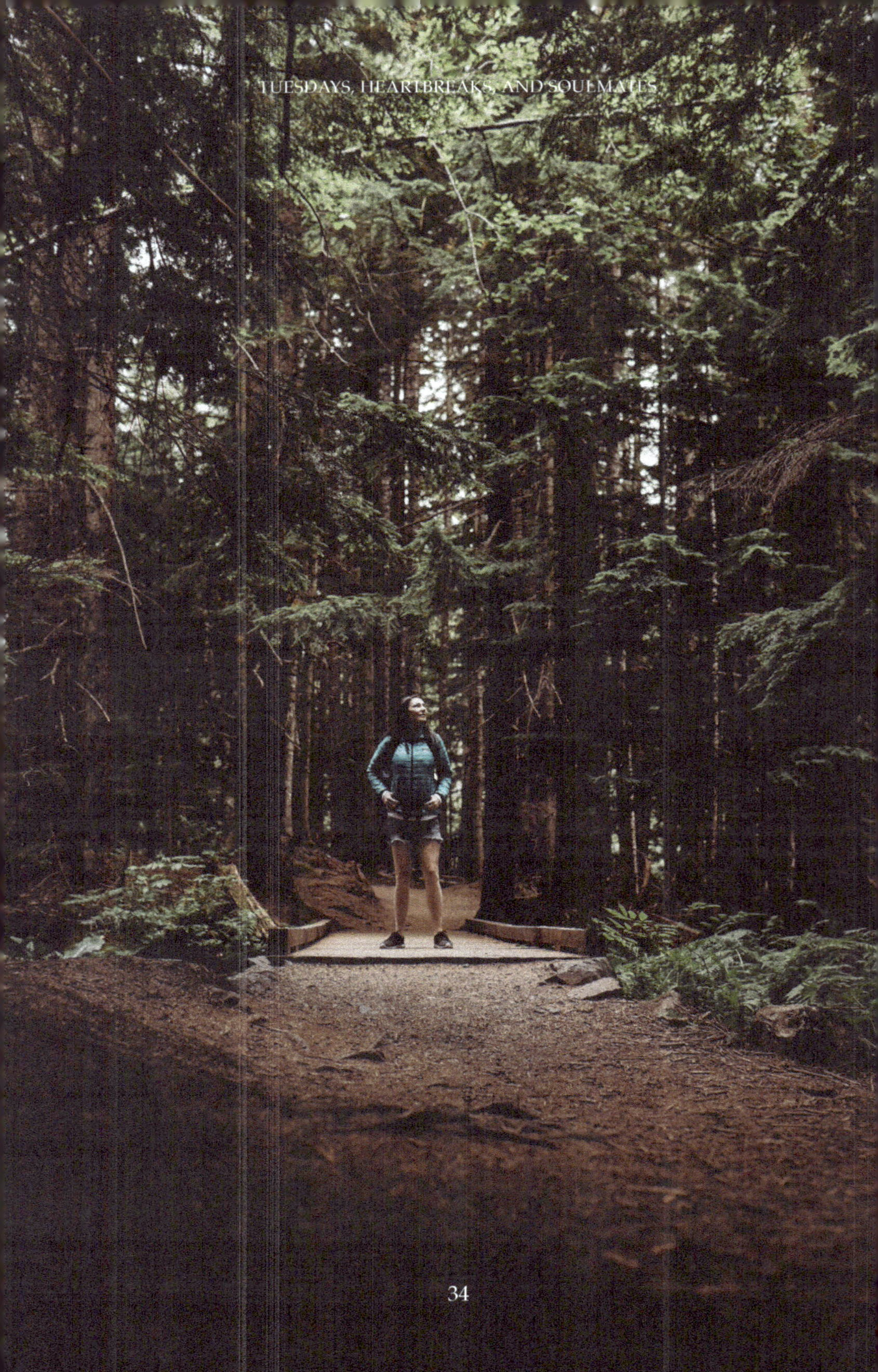

Searching for pieces of me in others
Sometimes friends and sometimes lovers
Time reveals the whole already within
Rejoicing in the comfort of my own skin

Exploring solitude and my higher purpose
Discovering self-reflection in lyrical verses
And in Mother Nature's churches

Navigating a journey through the shadow self
Promising never to put my heart back on the shelf
Seeing both light and dark when I meditate
Vowing never to let my truth dissipate

Healing wounds and authentically creating
Peaceful farewells to persuasion and debating
Intuition leading me to all that is awaiting

Daydreaming of a future partnership
Built with unwavering craftsmanship
I close my eyes and feel our embrace
Fast-forwarding to our fated time and space

The day will come for our flesh to collide
A destined connection finally aligned
Balanced masculine and feminine energy divine

Unveiling all of me shaped by profound depth
Finding home in the rise and fall of his breath
Our light will reflect of metaphysical prism
And we will forever dance to the rhythm

Of a song so sacred, two souls fully *awakened*

Love is in the way I take my coffee
each sip drowning me in memories
reflections of a time and space
I hold near and dear to my heart

Love is the records I put on
lyrics of a stranger's experiences
and I am convinced were written
to guide my soul home

Love is moments spent in solitude
learning the ins and outs of my being
truths that were hidden from the world
to fit into a place I was never meant be

Love is in the mountaintops—
canyons, deserts, and ocean waves
Mother Earth feels as one within
enlightenment found in these lands

Love is the arms that hold us long before we go
those that remain in the shadows of our past
those that show up and choose us today
those that are on their way in divine timing

Love is me. Love is you. Love is *everything*

Love is the basis of *all existence*

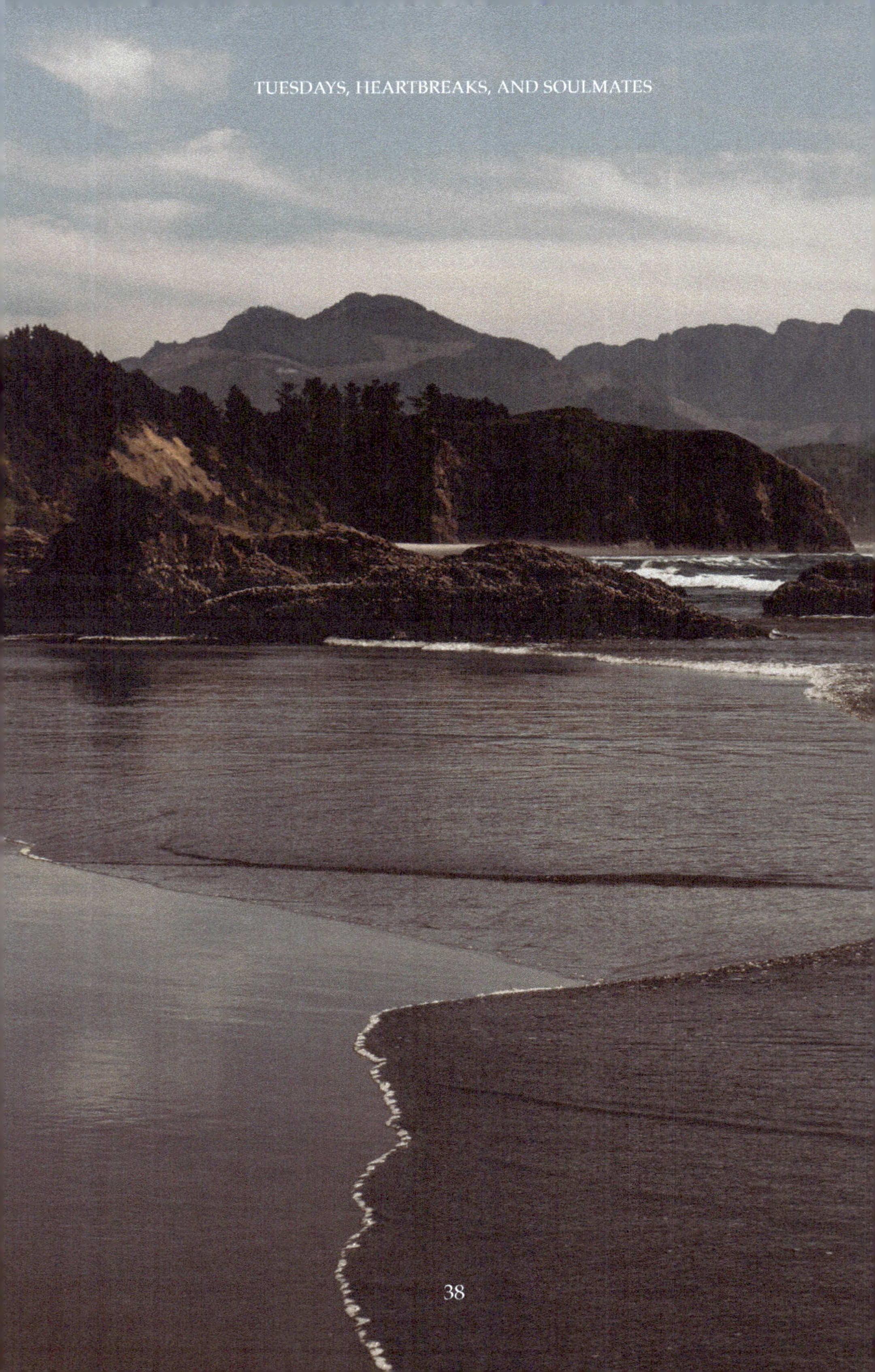

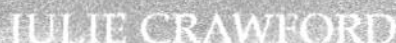

Tired of drowning in shallow experiences

She set sail into the *depths* of her soul

to discover the nature of true fulfillment

Dear Soulmate,

You are *scattered* throughout these pages
Read them knowing in some way they exist because
Our connection, even for just a brief moment in time
Brought awareness to fascinating versions of myself

Collision of an energy so familiar
Gospel of the stars reflecting in your eyes
Shining a facet of the jewel, no longer dim
Colliding as if all part of the plan

High octane fuel for the road ahead
Chapter in the story of my becoming
The fundamentals of love unraveling
Planting perennials in the garden of life

When you could no longer stay, I let go
Holding on to the essence of *you*
Like an element in my atmosphere
Living forever in and around me

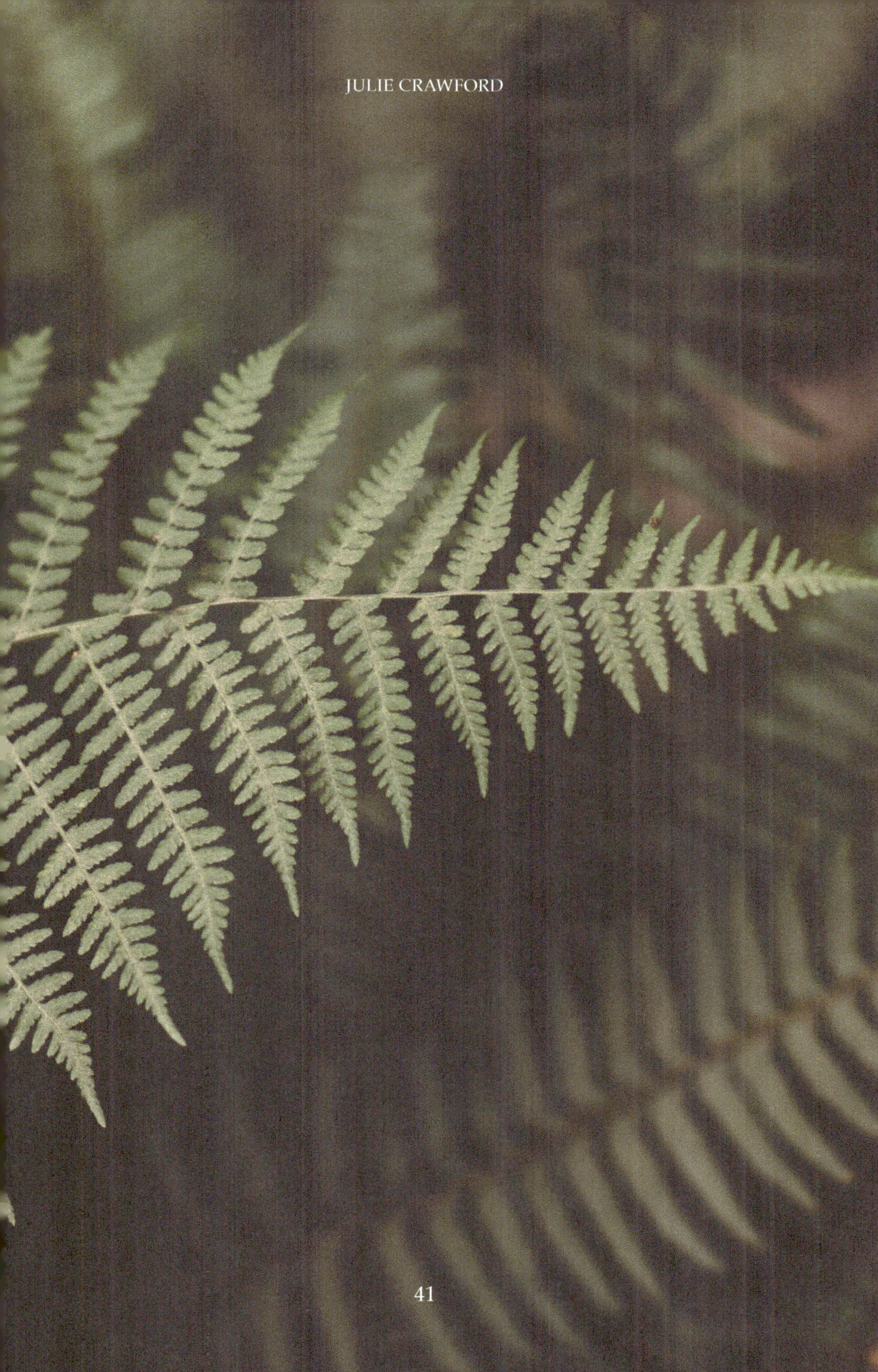

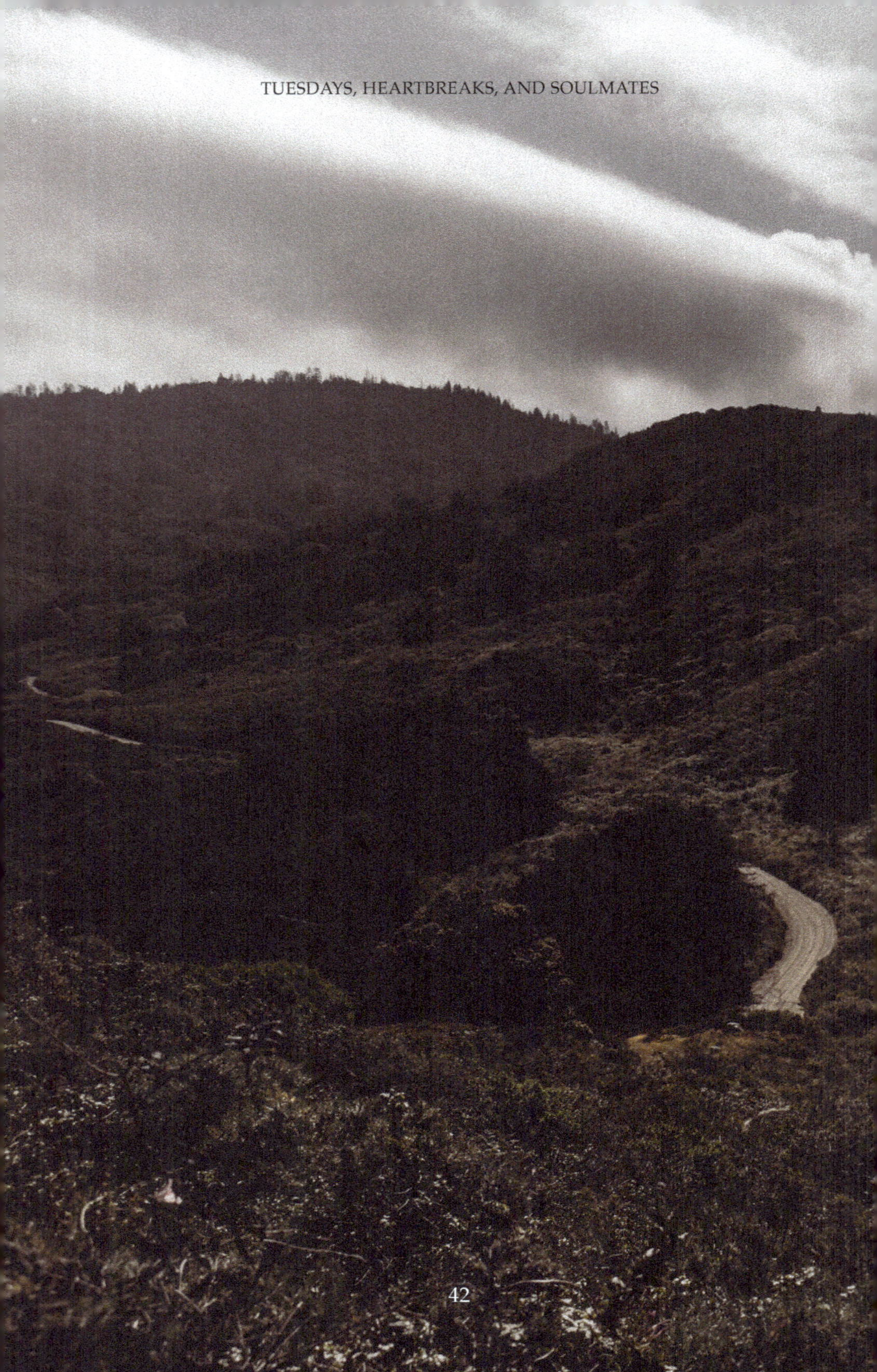

She learns to navigate an adventurous life

Harmonizing with the splendid twists and turns

of a journey she is *proud* to call hers

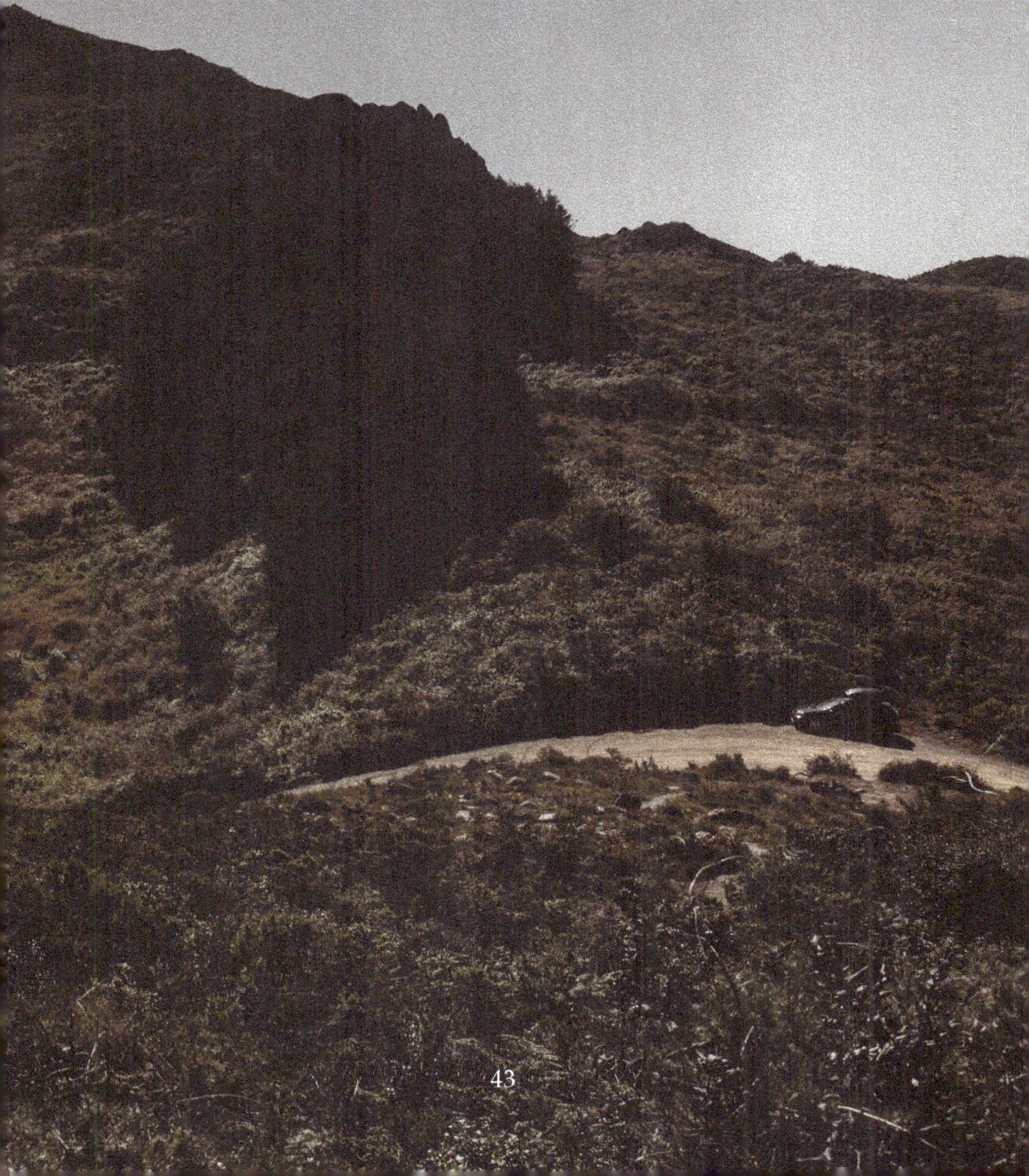

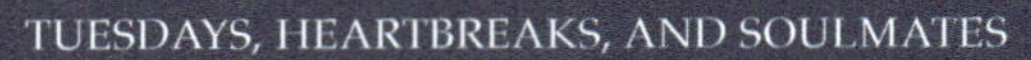

learning to swim

I will not sacrifice the greatest parts of my soul

watering down versions of a divinely crafted self

until I am left drowning in an ocean of remorse

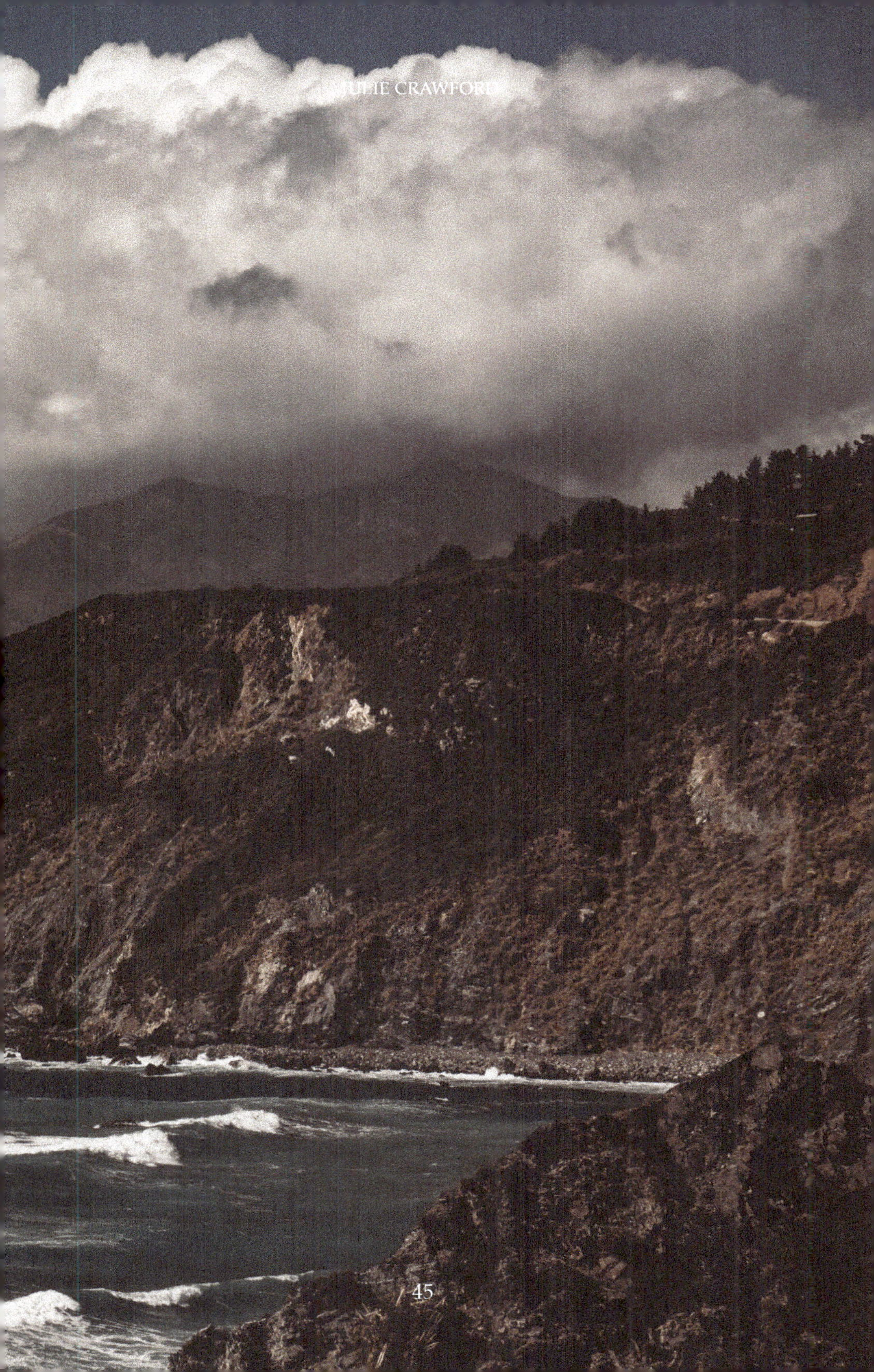
JULIE CRAWFORD

She drove across the country

to the Rocky Mountains

the snowy hills of Colorado

you once promised her

Letting go of everything

no longer serving her truth

the *wholesome* self

She promises herself

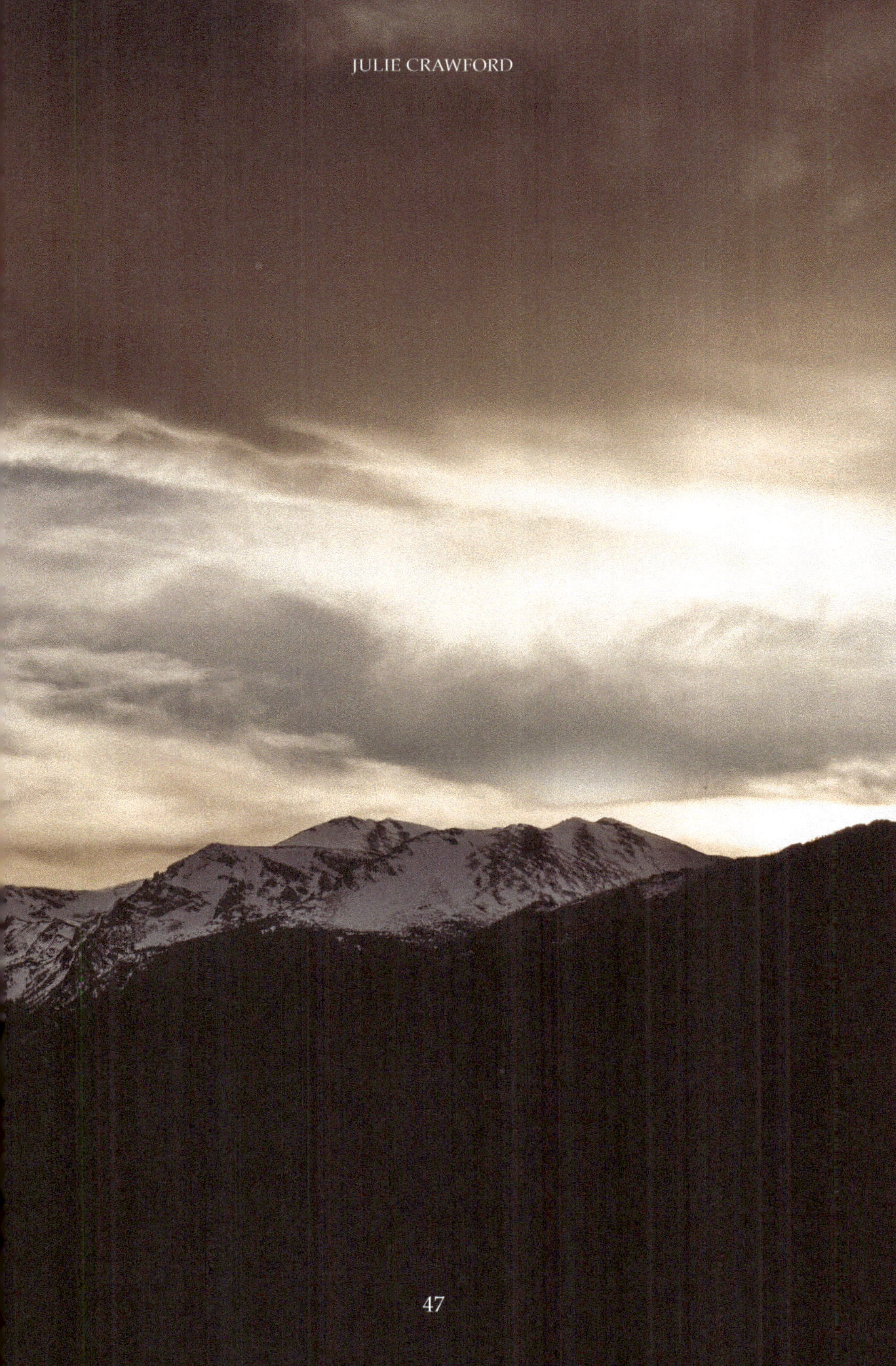

Past versions of myself struggled with finding purpose

I would search endlessly for passion that felt whole

try new approaches, think I have it, feel lost again

and the *wheel* would just keep on spinning

Through a conscious choice to search within

I learned that diving into emotional depth

being present, transparent with myself

are crucial for soul-level fulfillment

I want out of my time on Earth

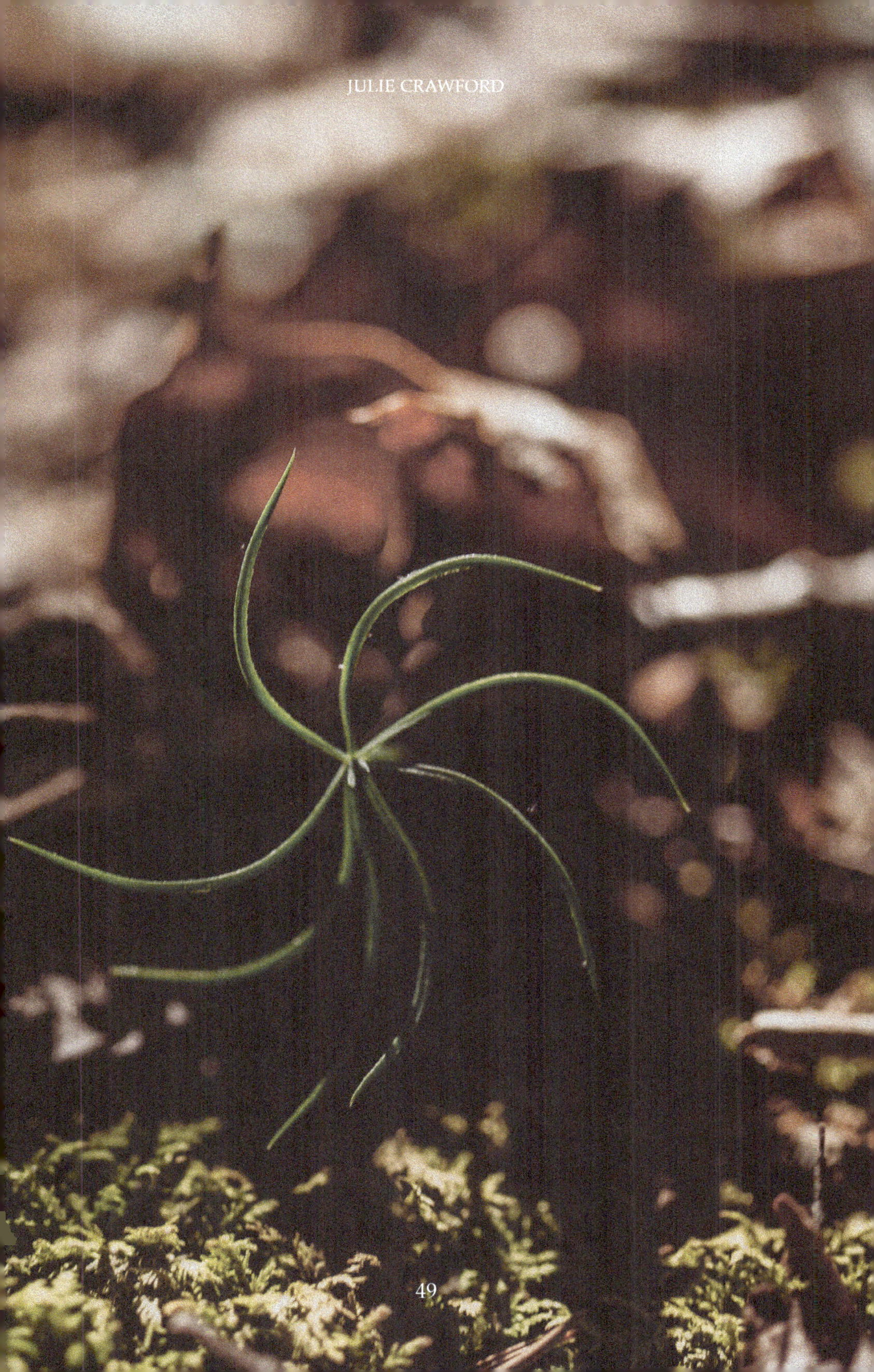
JULIE CRAWFORD

Gentle Ones, you were the break
the lifting of clouds once covering
my skies like a wounded overcast

Sweet Loves, you were the break
the rays of light shining through the
somber fog warming my frosted heart

Dear Angels, you were my break
the awakening truth of a brighter side
reaching high above skies of *gray*

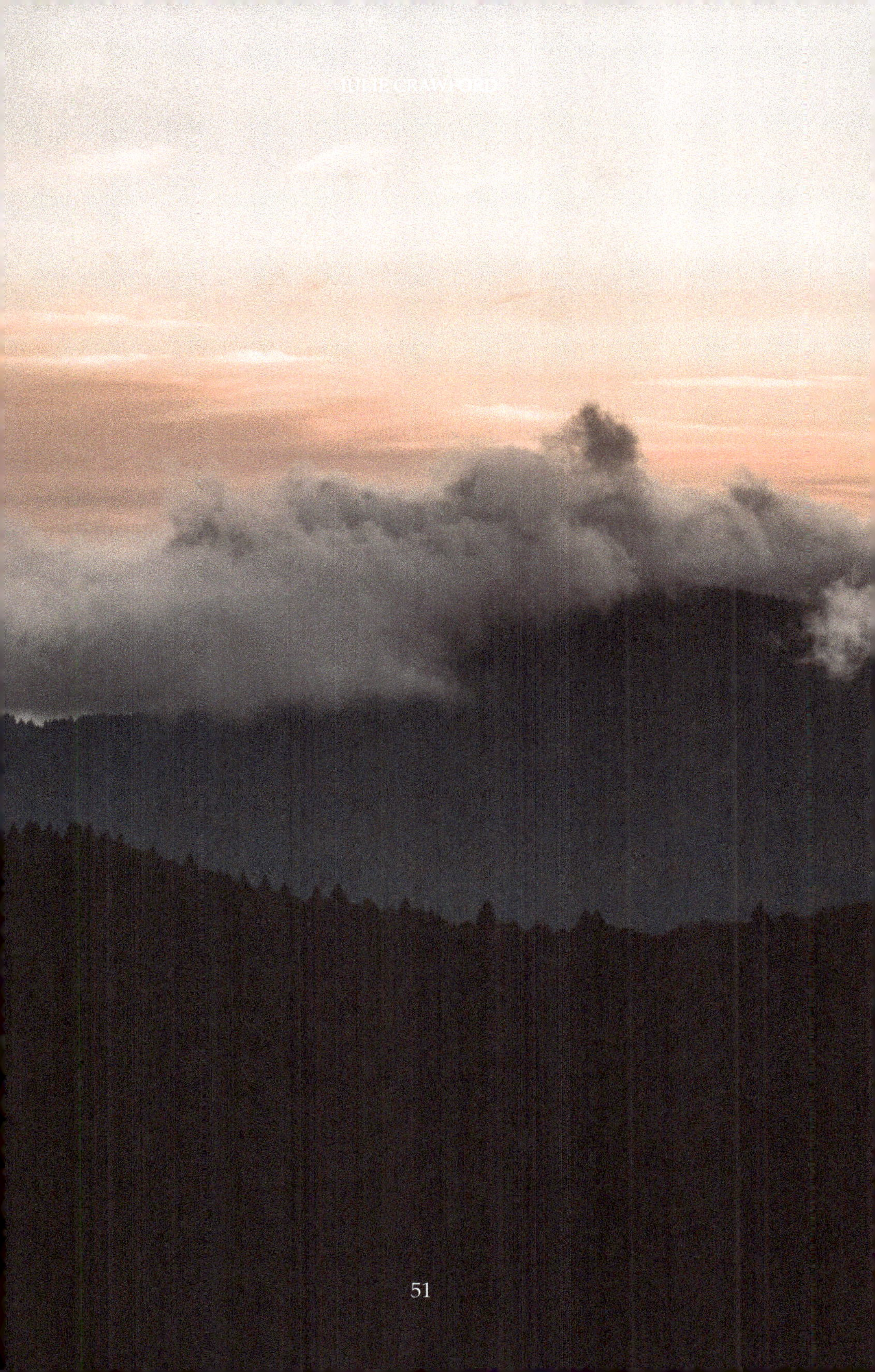

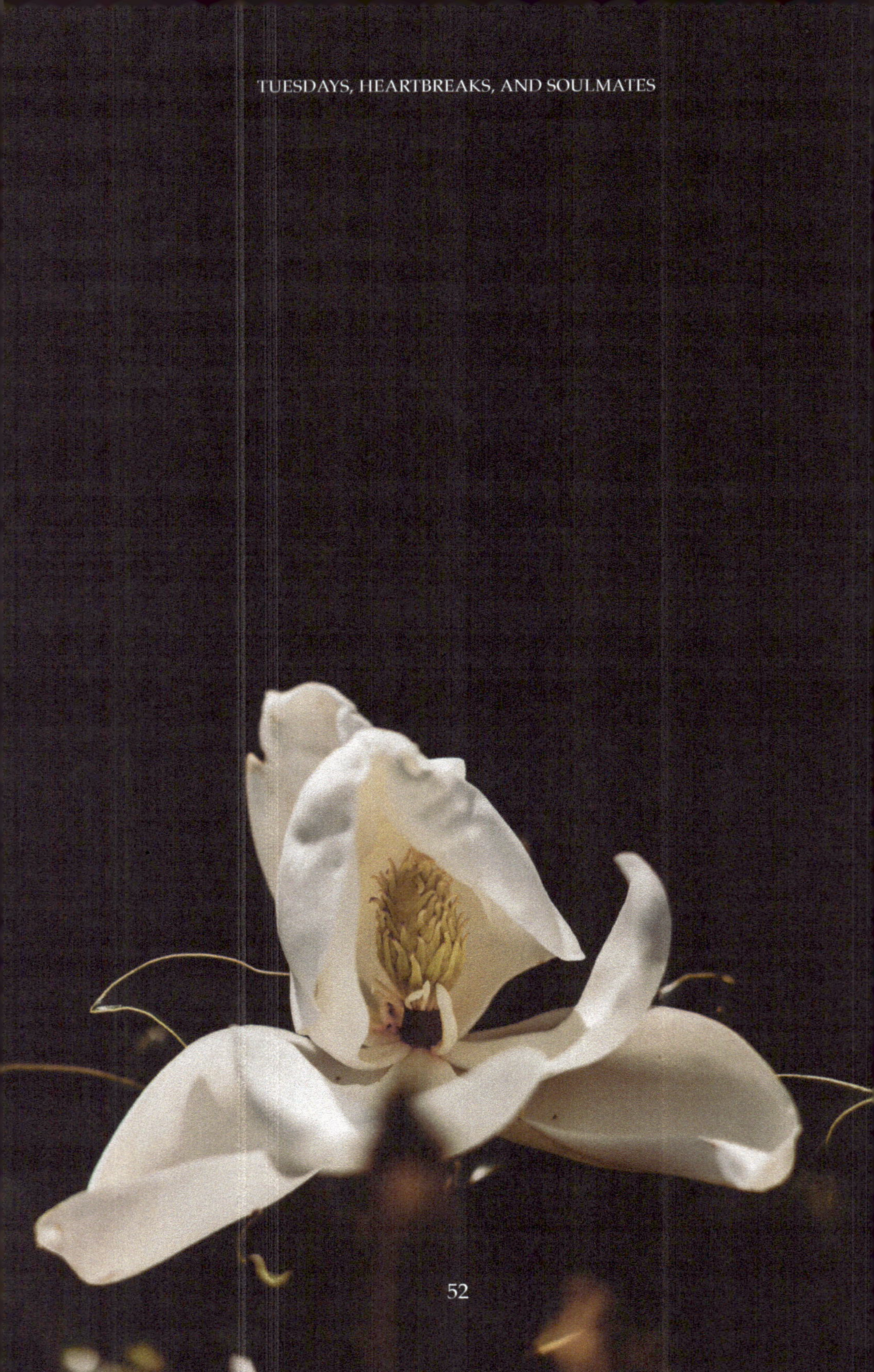

Traveling has proven itself capable of

unfolding layers of the inner self

Each new journey reveals a greater

awareness of myself and all that surrounds

—an exquisite *blossoming* of my soul

Goodbye to anything less than I deserve to have
Goodbye to trying to convince others of my worth
Goodbye to anyone unwilling to choose me
Goodbye to folks who think I am too much
Goodbye to losing myself in codependency
Goodbye to repeating old patterns over and over

Farewell, I have made peace with my *shadows*

I welcome all meant for this beautifully crafted life—
energy that sets my soul on fire
loving relationships with people who show up
and stay
conversations with friends who listen attentively
even when my *long story short* is never really short
Phase 10 and taco Tuesdays
music awakening something a little deeper inside of me
lyrics guiding me along this ever-evolving journey
hikes that may kick my butt
making me stronger in every sense
synchronous fireflies
mountaintops with fairy wings and golden flowers
road trips to see a favorite artist with a friend knowing
they won't judge as I cry during the ones that move me
motherhood
family that I could never disappoint because
"Everything you'll ever be, you already are to me"
moments amidst the wild
writing with intention and depth
purposeful living
walks along the river, ripped hammocks
unconditional love
the life-partnership destined to align
Home

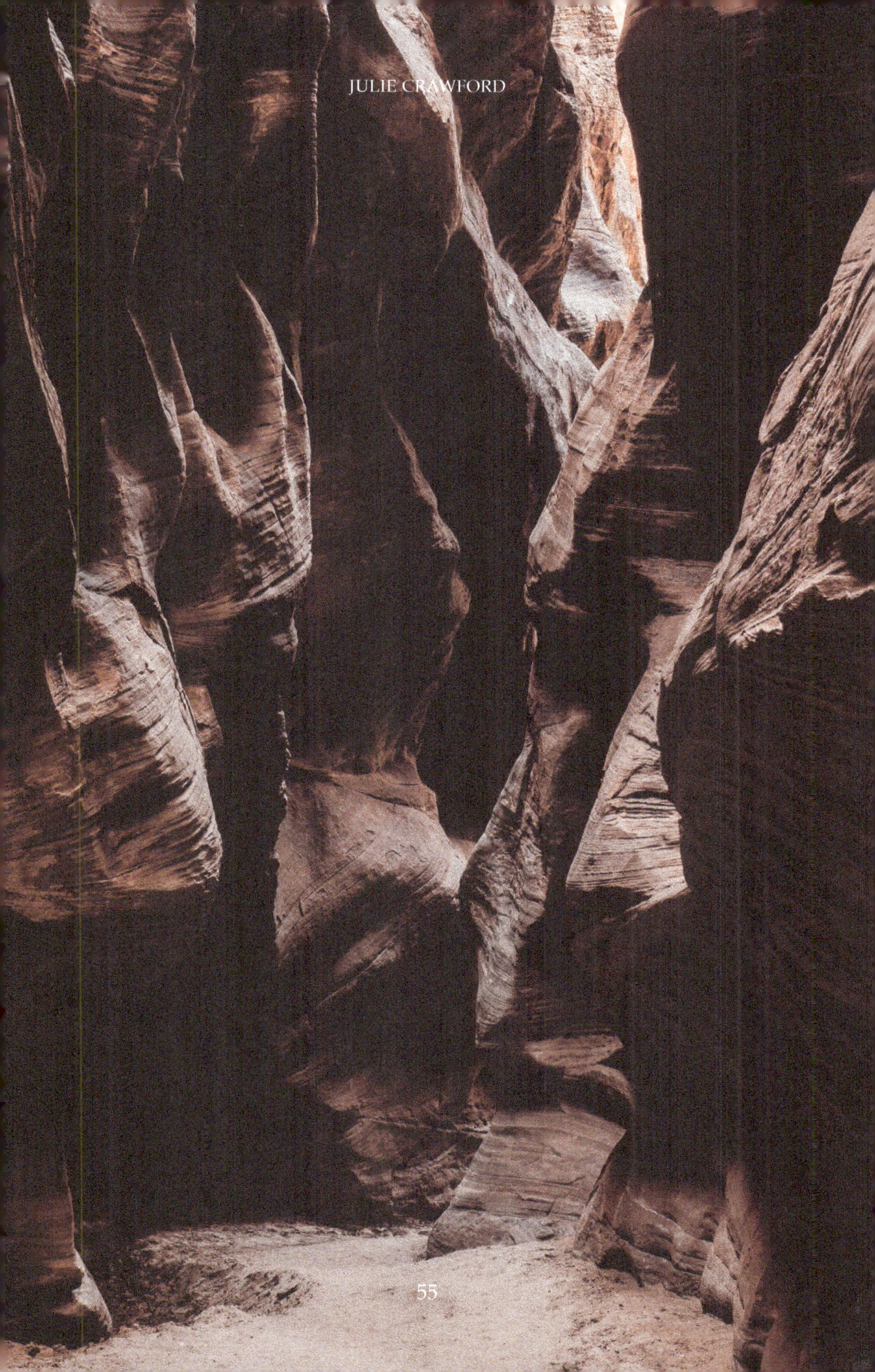
JULIE CRAWFORD

Lay-flat seats cradle me while I sleep in the wilderness
Steering wheel grips tight to my hands through
Deserts, mountains, coasts, and even busy cities
as I learn to navigate the maps of my own heart

Enclosed by four doors, space exists for me to
continually grow as my most authentic self

I am never judged for my ideas or talking aloud to myself
I am never asked to bring my singing from a level 10 to a 2
nor do I hear complaining when I play the same song
eight times in a row because I crave the resonating lyrics

Sometimes I cry uncontrollably
other times I laugh out loud
I will admit many times I do both at the same time

I have been scared shitless without
a person in sight or phone service—
bathed, cooked meals, and overcome fear
lost, found peace, and ultimately come alive

All inside of my *sanctified* place

JULIE CRAWFORD

In a world that is easy to lose yourself in

feeding into meaningless expectations

drowning your soul in the chaotic mess

I challenge you to *rise* above

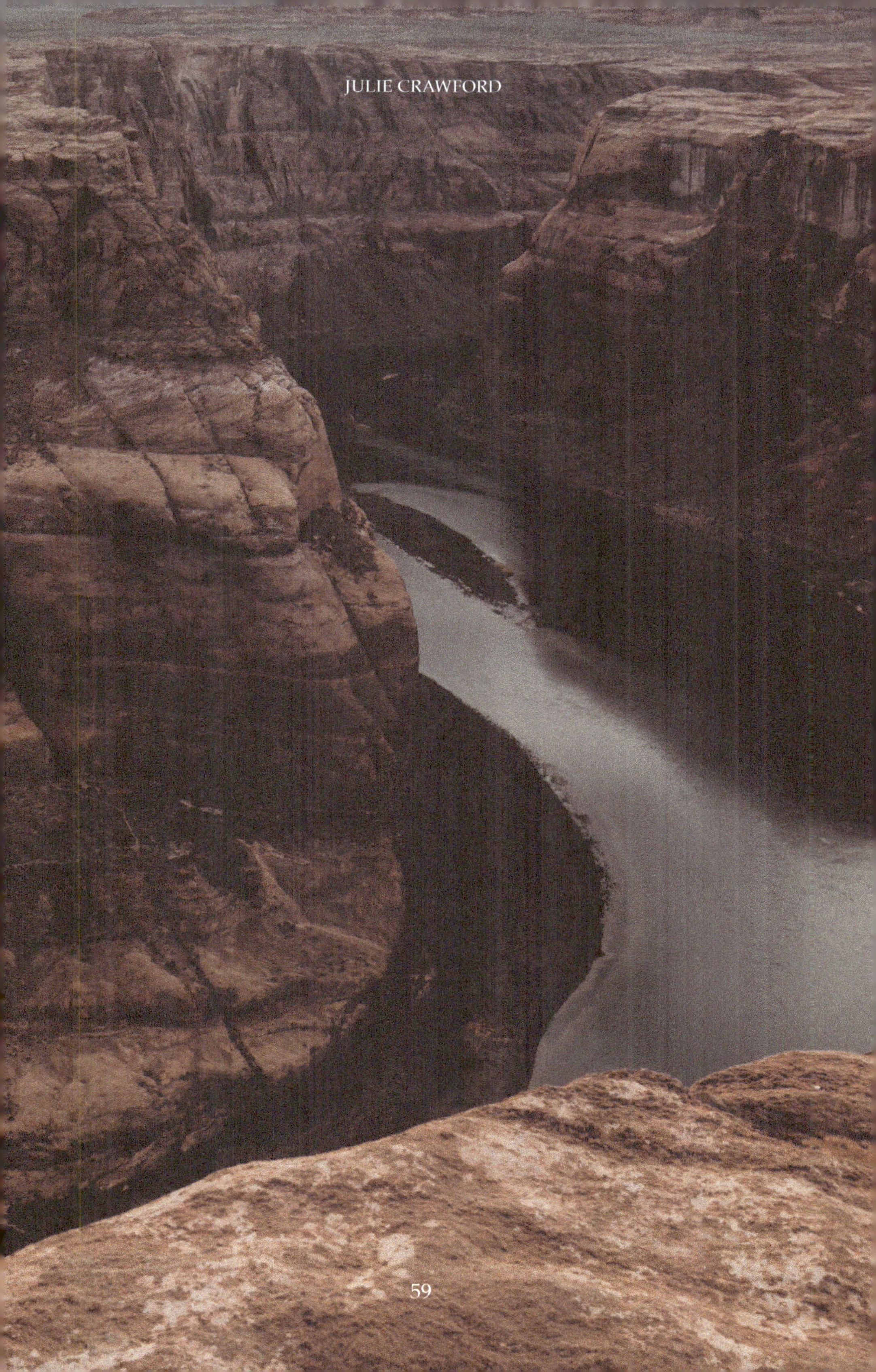
JULIE CRAWFORD

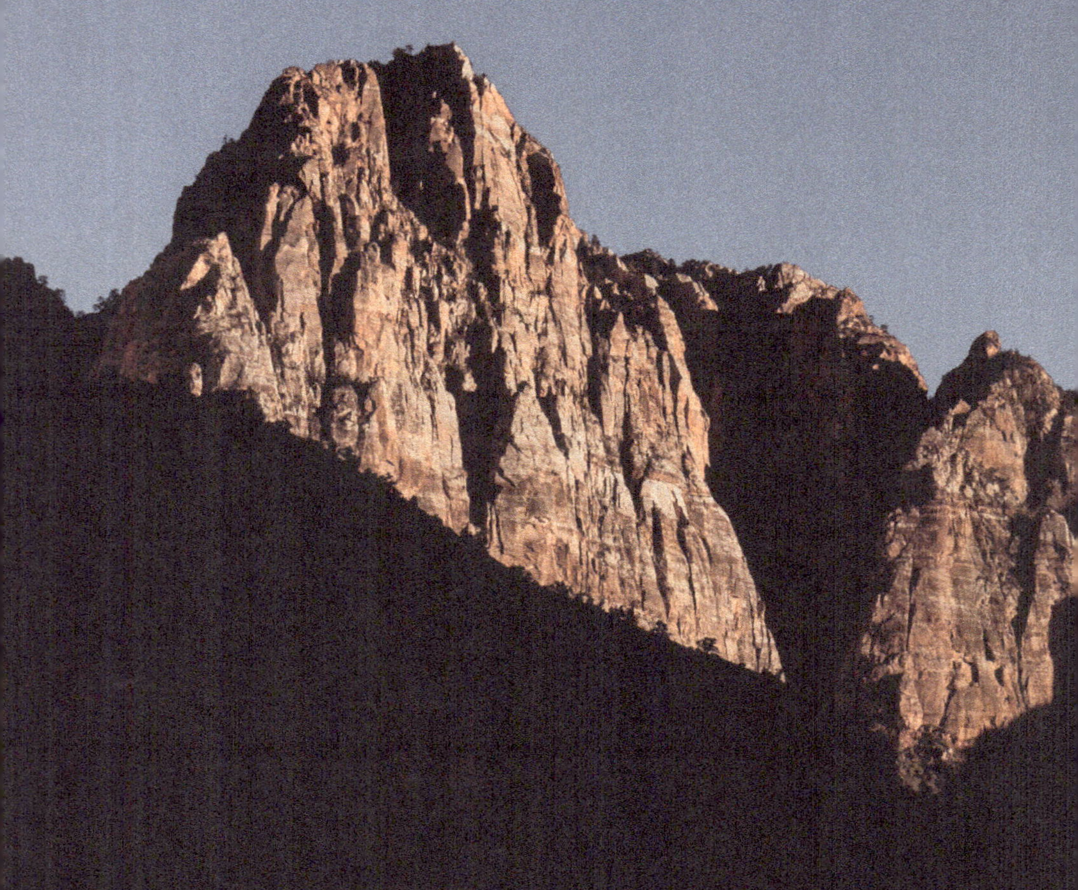

One of the most
beautiful gifts
is the giving of
our most *honest* self

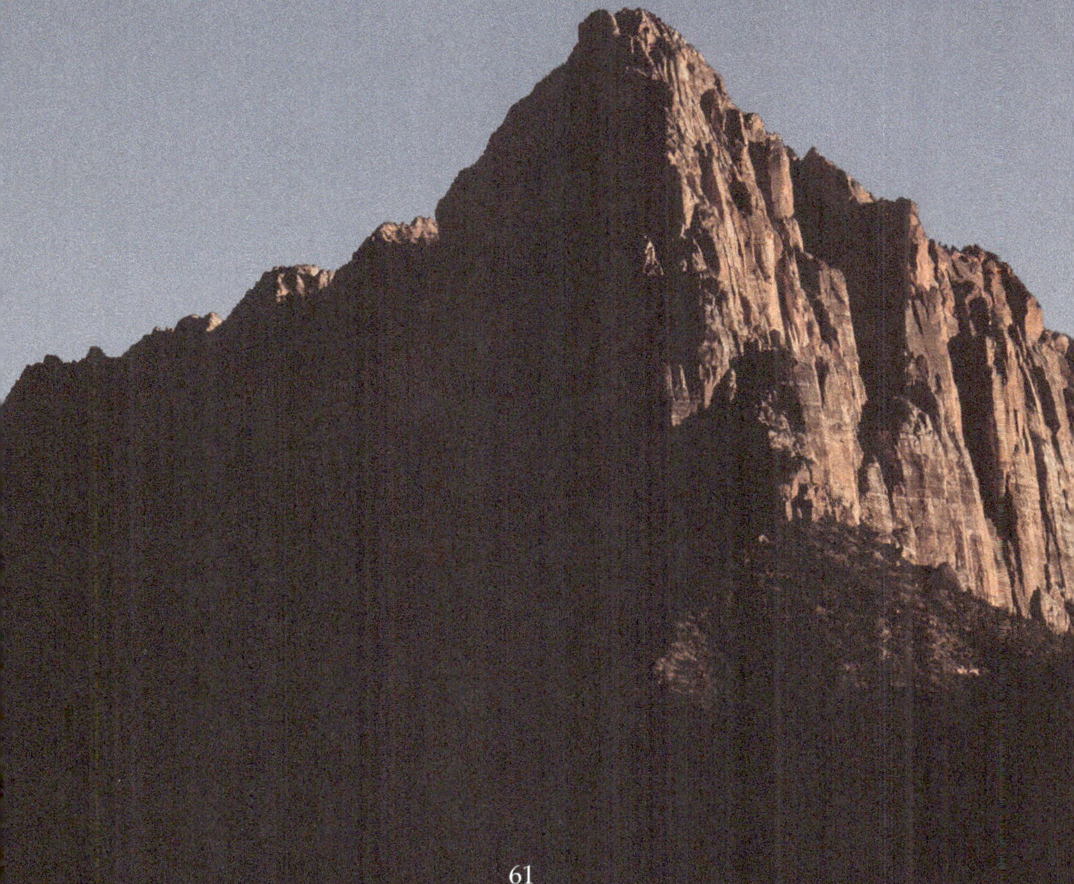

We've danced a thousand cosmic journeys

Lifetimes of finding our way back together

Our souls bound by metaphysical *gravity*

Colliding in the sacred force known as love

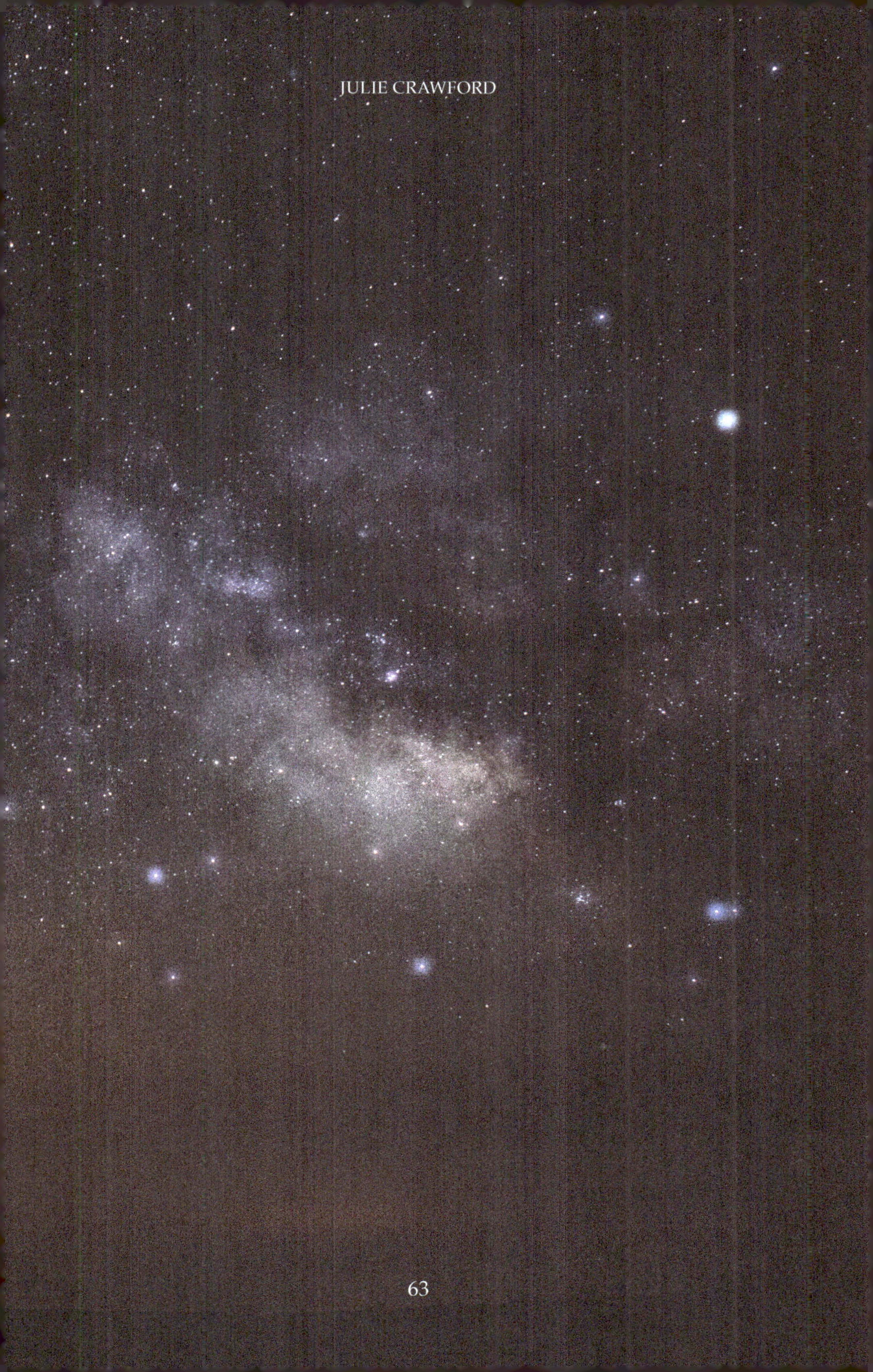

Open the door.

on the pilot's spoken command
three words, and I resist the urge
to hold on to the nearest anything
the door lifts towards the wing
a gust of wind chills the air
awareness hits at warp speed

stepping out on the ledge
at the mercy of fate
staring deep into the unknown
for the first time in my life
zero expectations of what
the next moment brings

Fearlessly present
and ready to experience
the high at 14,000 feet

a *simple* little kind of free

Falling

Earth suspended in time
waiting for the return of
a soul only ever wanting
to feel something real

spiraling into a backflip
eyes open and heart open
360° views paint around me
showing what exists within

deep red canyons
snowcapped mountains
carved space for adventure
climbs that lead to the highest self

breathtaking plunge to my divine path
no more holding myself back, I let go
120 mph with arms stretched wide
Releasing all shadowing my truth

I hit the ground *running*

Chasing me

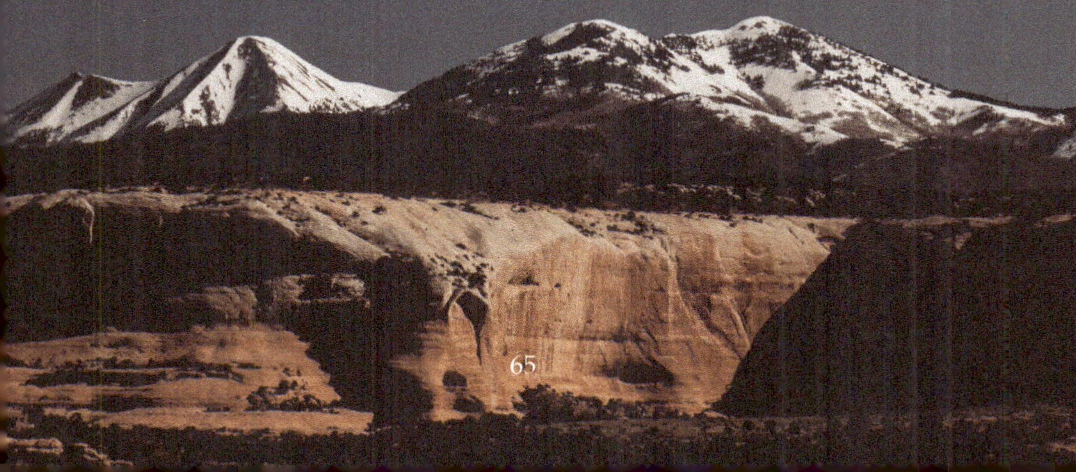

I lovingly *surrender* the pieces

that hold me back from becoming everything

I am meant to be

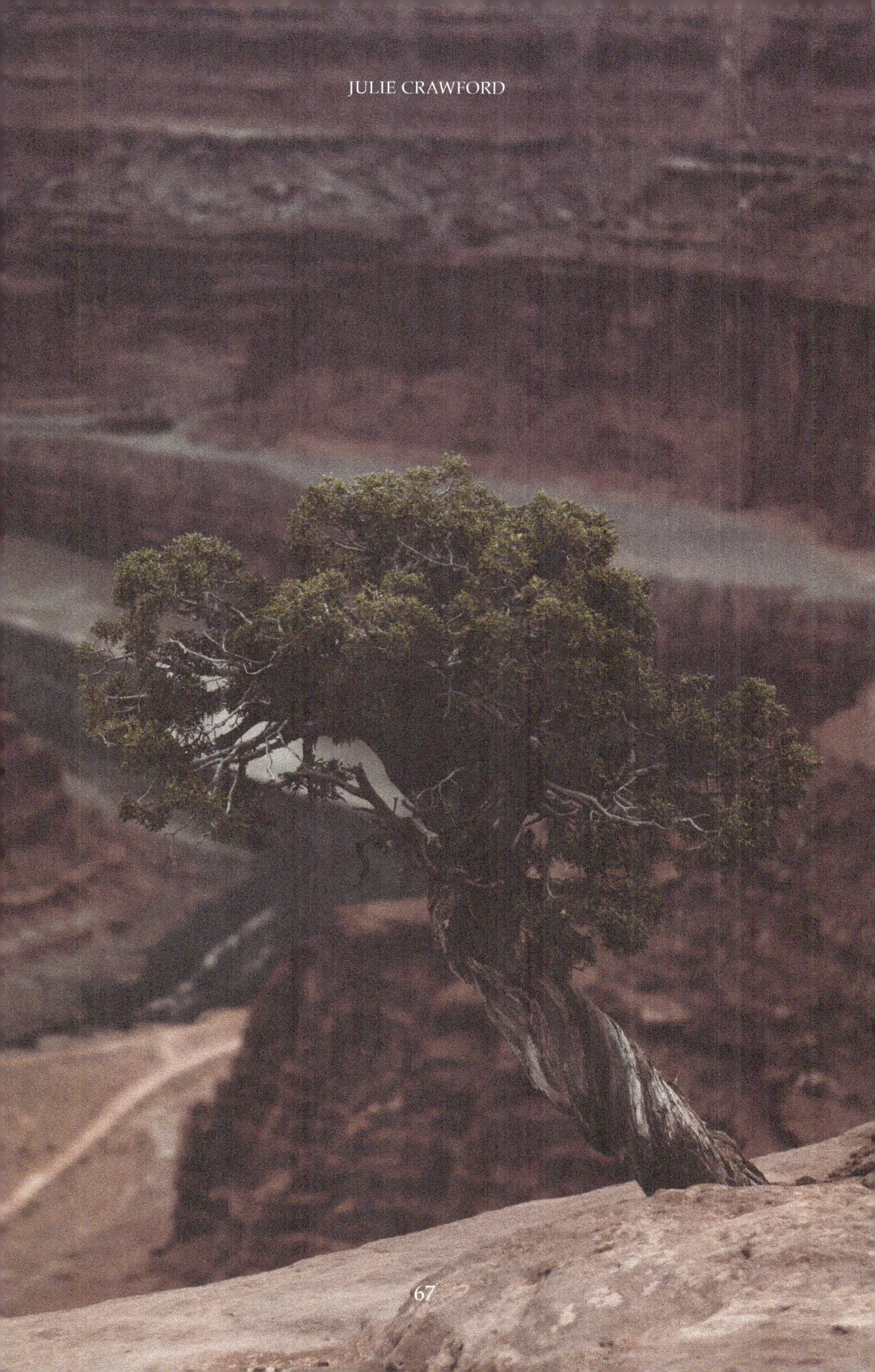

Peace raining down over us
Embracing within sleeping bags
Sweet slumber outside the tent
Dreaming under a blanket of stars
with a soulful love to keep us warm
That marvelous night, time stood still
and you held me softly in a space
that will forever be *ours*

She fell in love with the sunrise
The way the soft light holds her—
all of her

The rest of the world quiet
Daystar beginning to shine
Sun-drenched euphoria
Treasured morning rituals
Playing vinyl records
Creating art and mindful chaos
Meditating and stretching
Welcoming the brilliance
Spiritual epiphanies
Turning life into poetry

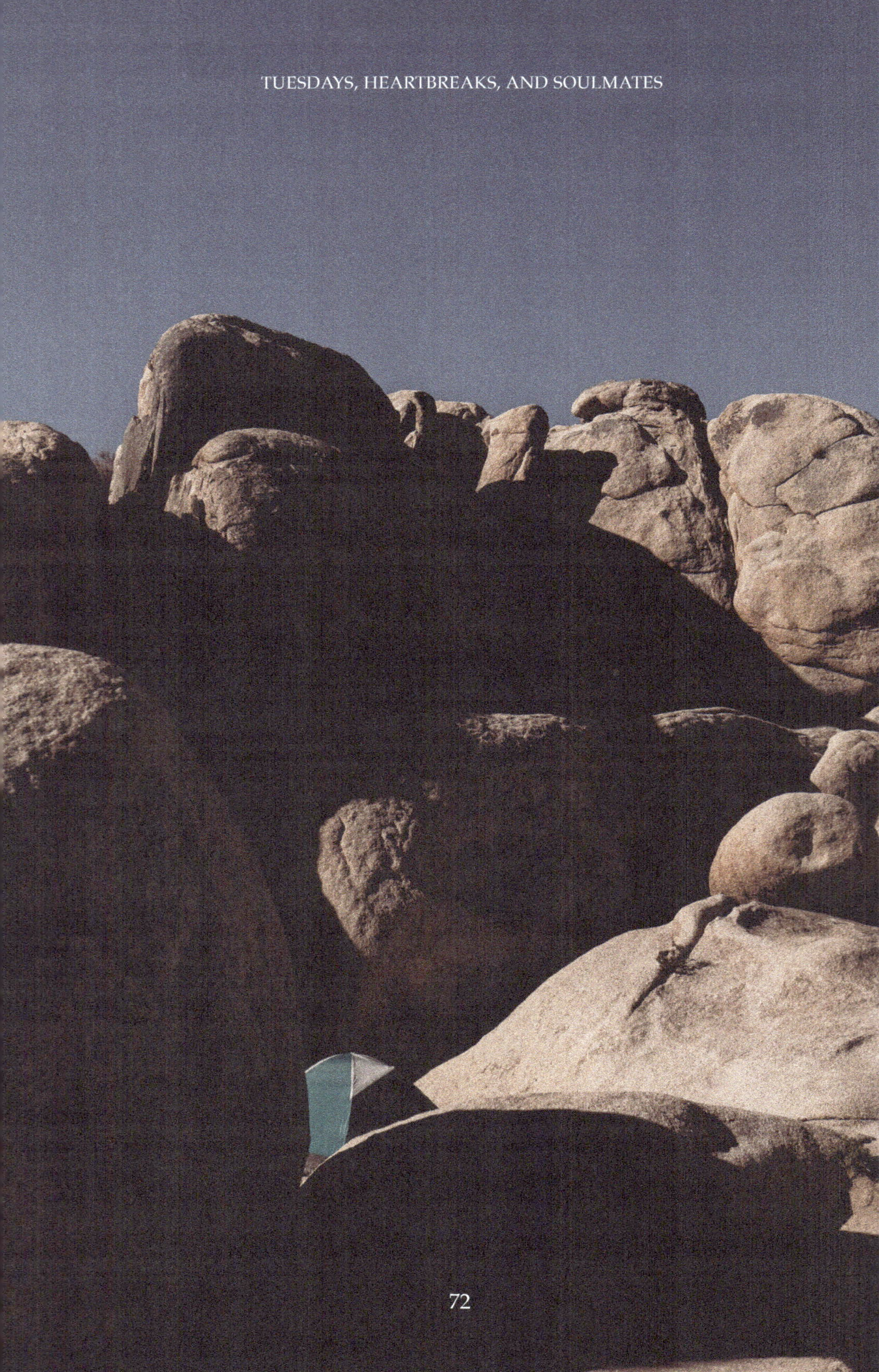

After years of shadow work and celibacy

Exploring to find answers, not told by others

I became an architect of my own path

Learning how not to be scared to walk alone

Isolating to create space for my own thoughts

to exist without clutter from external chaos

All to find my way to back to my loving self

I found a home among the *larks*
Embracing hope, joy, and laughter
and singing with the sunrise
Crescent upon your breast
Feminine comfort of the moon
You make me feel safe
to show up as my whole self
Never feeling the desire to hide
Unconditional love and support
in good times and the tough ones
You know stories behind these pages
—poems and photography
—the chaos and the art
Tales I have never shared with another
Always in my corner, having my back
Nourishing creativity
Evolving to my fullest potential
You hold space for me to unfold
Listening and asking the hard questions
Challenging me to expand further
Shining boldly in your truth
Strength to keep me reaching higher
You provide a peaceful shelter
to retreat and recharge my soul
You know me all too well
and love me more for it
Through you, I am learning the
true meaning of friendship

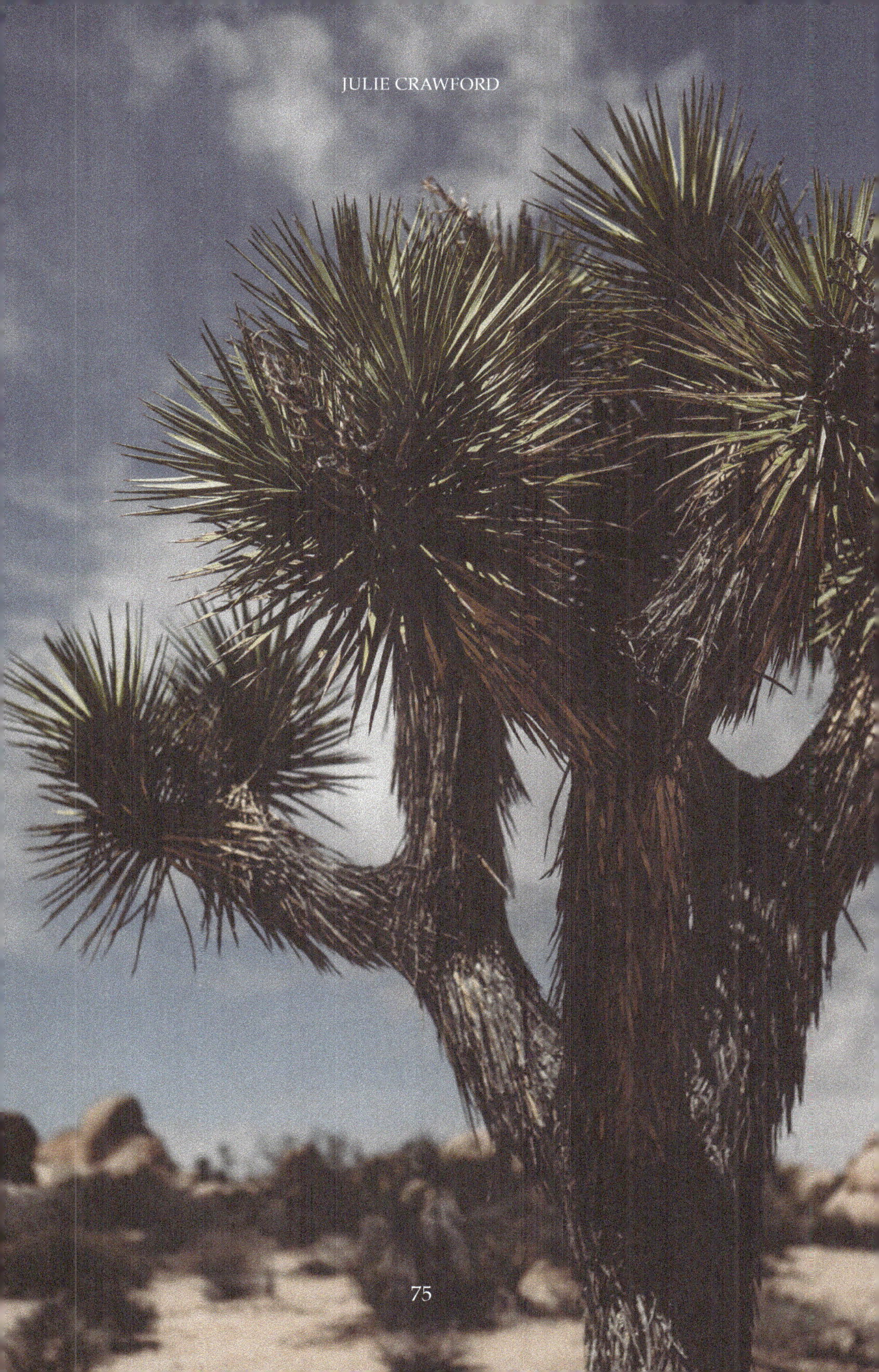

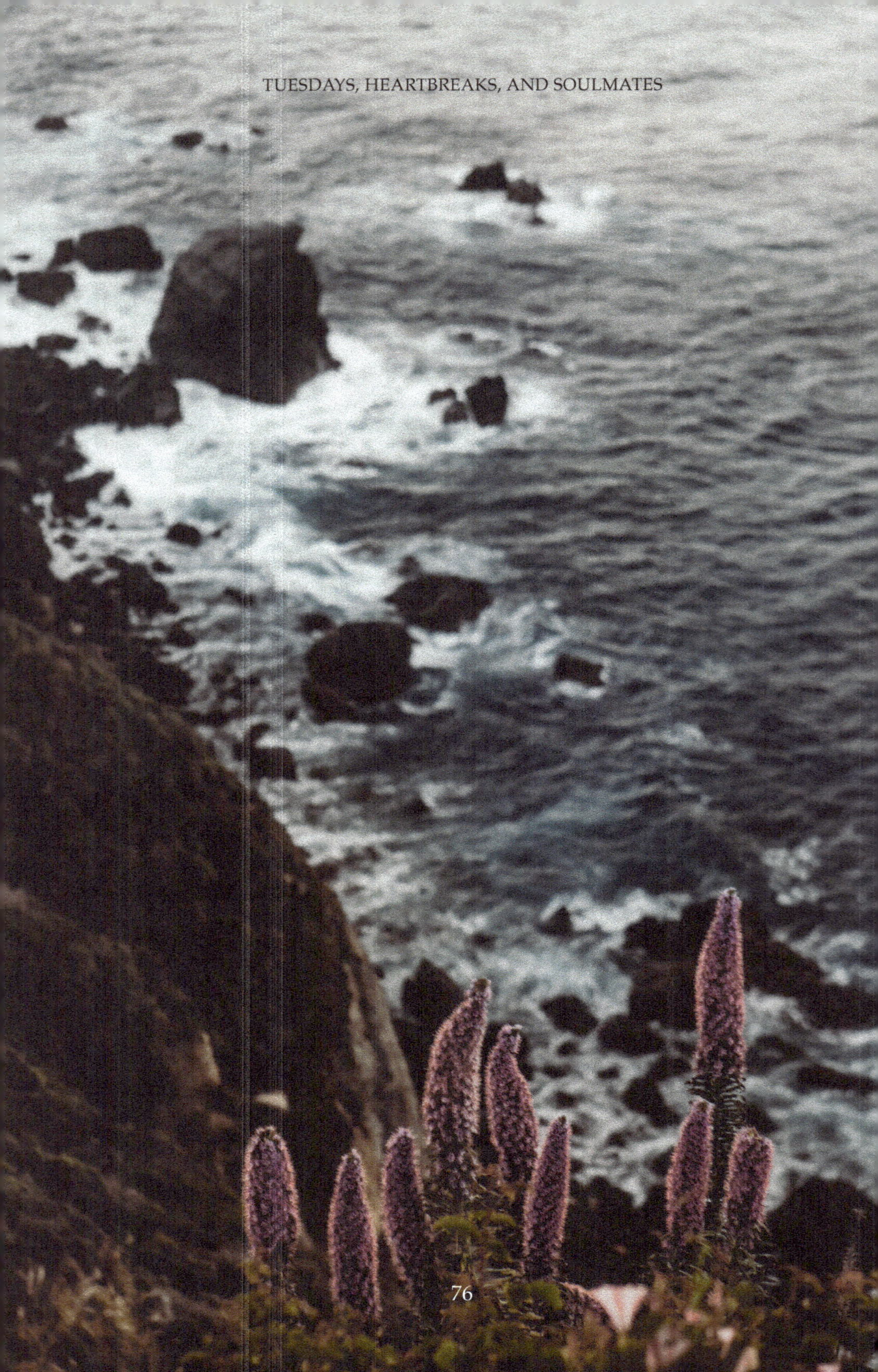

(blackout "Dear Marie" lyrics by John Mayer)

Vulnerability creates *intimacy*

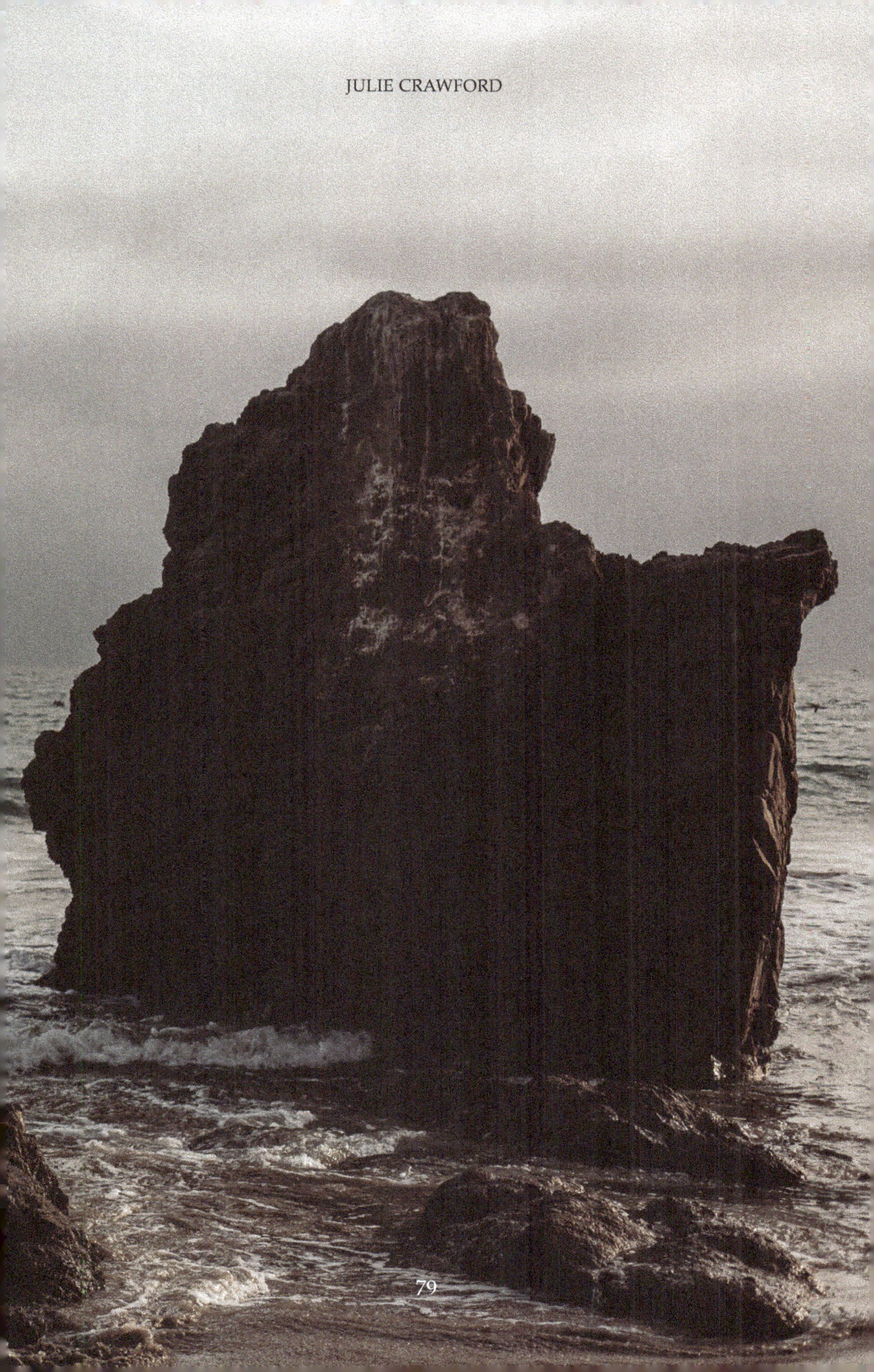

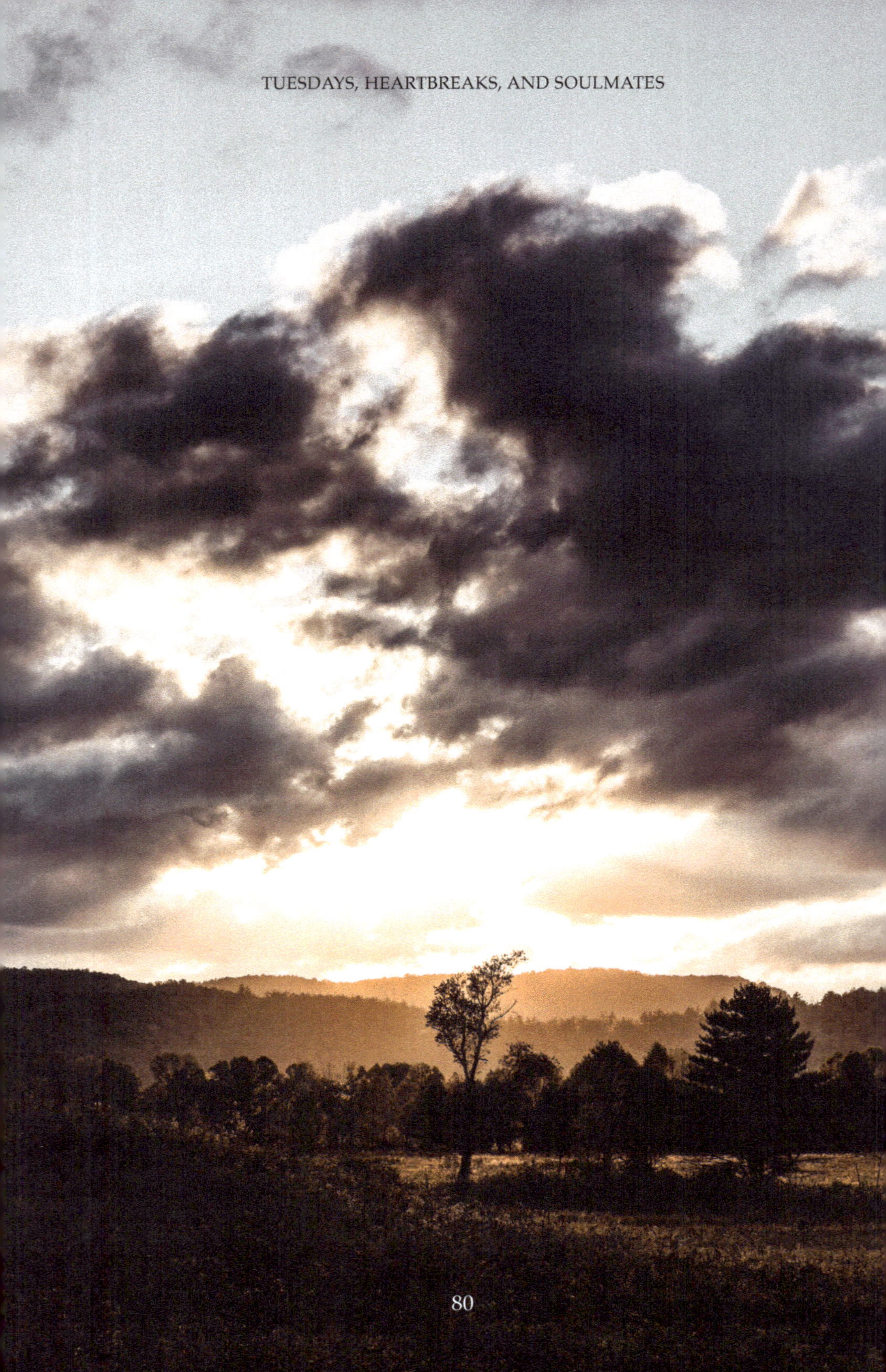

Glow settling below

Distant peaks

Our lips collide

Tasting adventure

This is the start of

Something *astonishing*

You showed me the lighthouse
and painted silhouettes in my sky
You had the first glimpse of
the person I was becoming
Open and vulnerable
I discovered a captivating self
through the reflection
that shined in your eyes
You held space for me
to expand beyond anything
I had ever imagined
I never told you how
through your genuineness
how you choose to show up
and your love and care for me
opened doors to a magnificent journey
finding deeper passion and purpose
I never thought the last time I seen you
would be the last time I seen you
Heart shattered into a thousand pieces
I picked up all my dearest facets
and kept moving forward
Reminiscing our connection
catapult on the path of self-discovery
and I am eternally grateful
even if I am only
dancing with your ghost
and the *memory* of your face

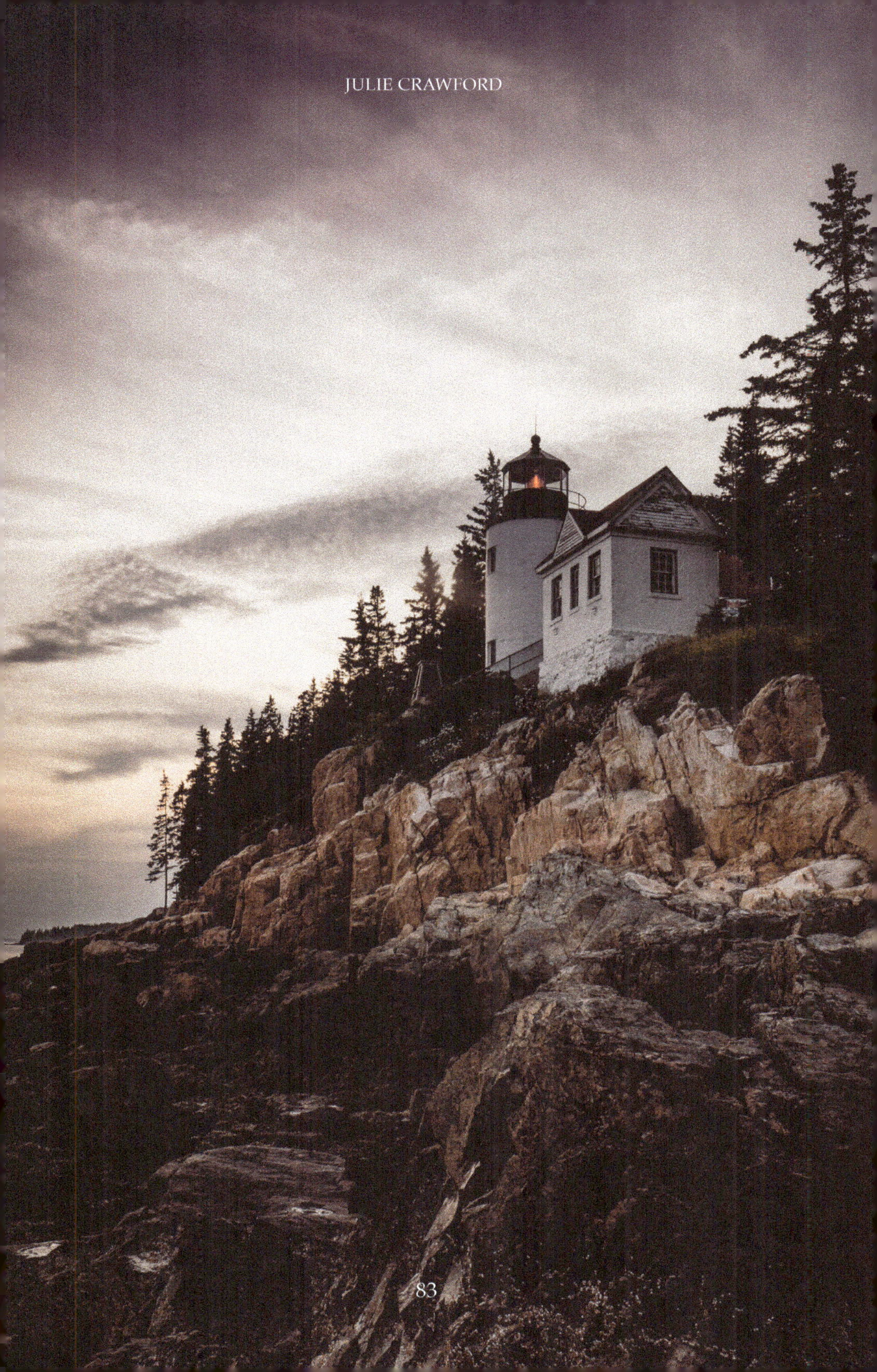
JULIE CRAWFORD

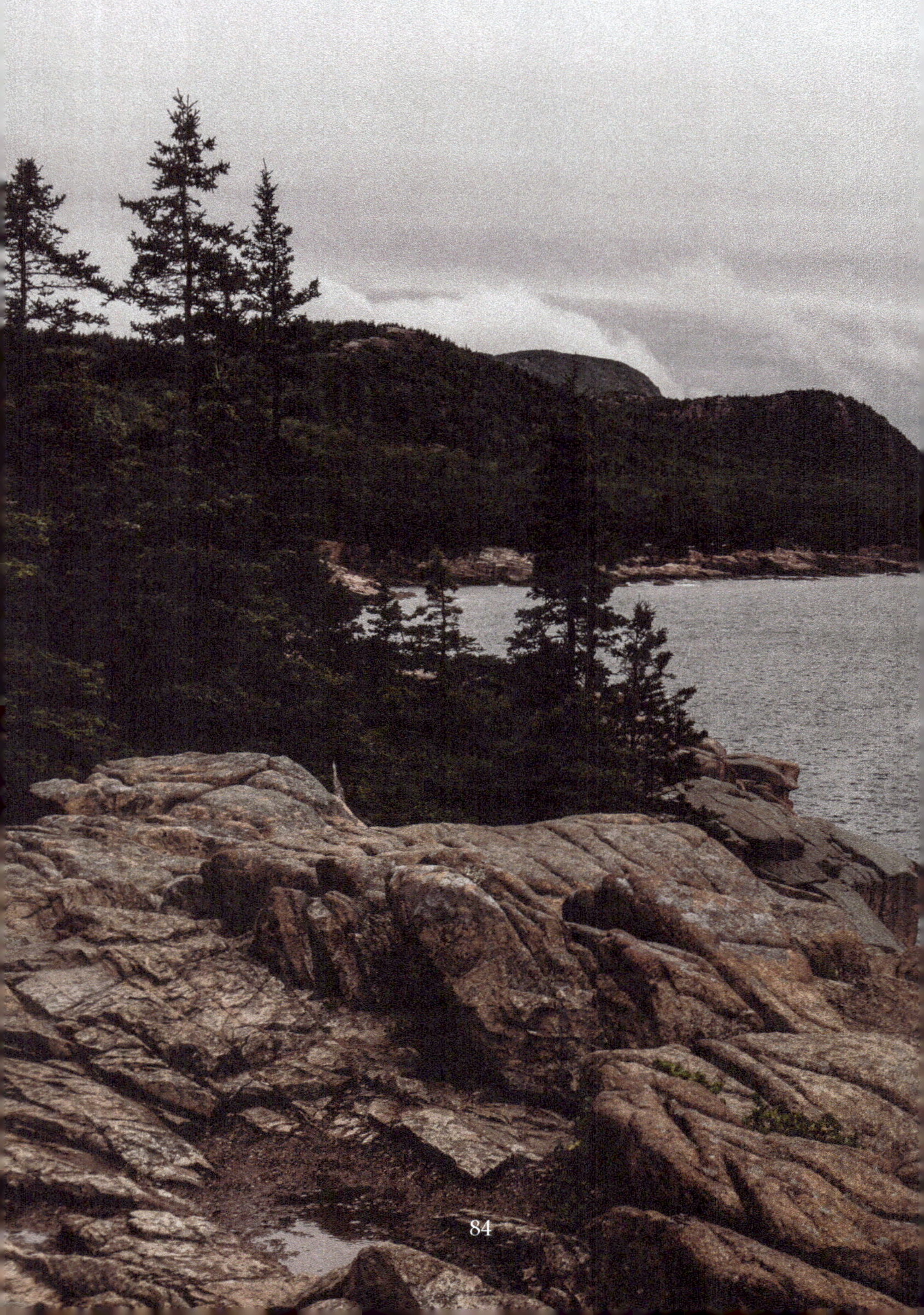

Just be your loving self

and I'll find my way *back to you*

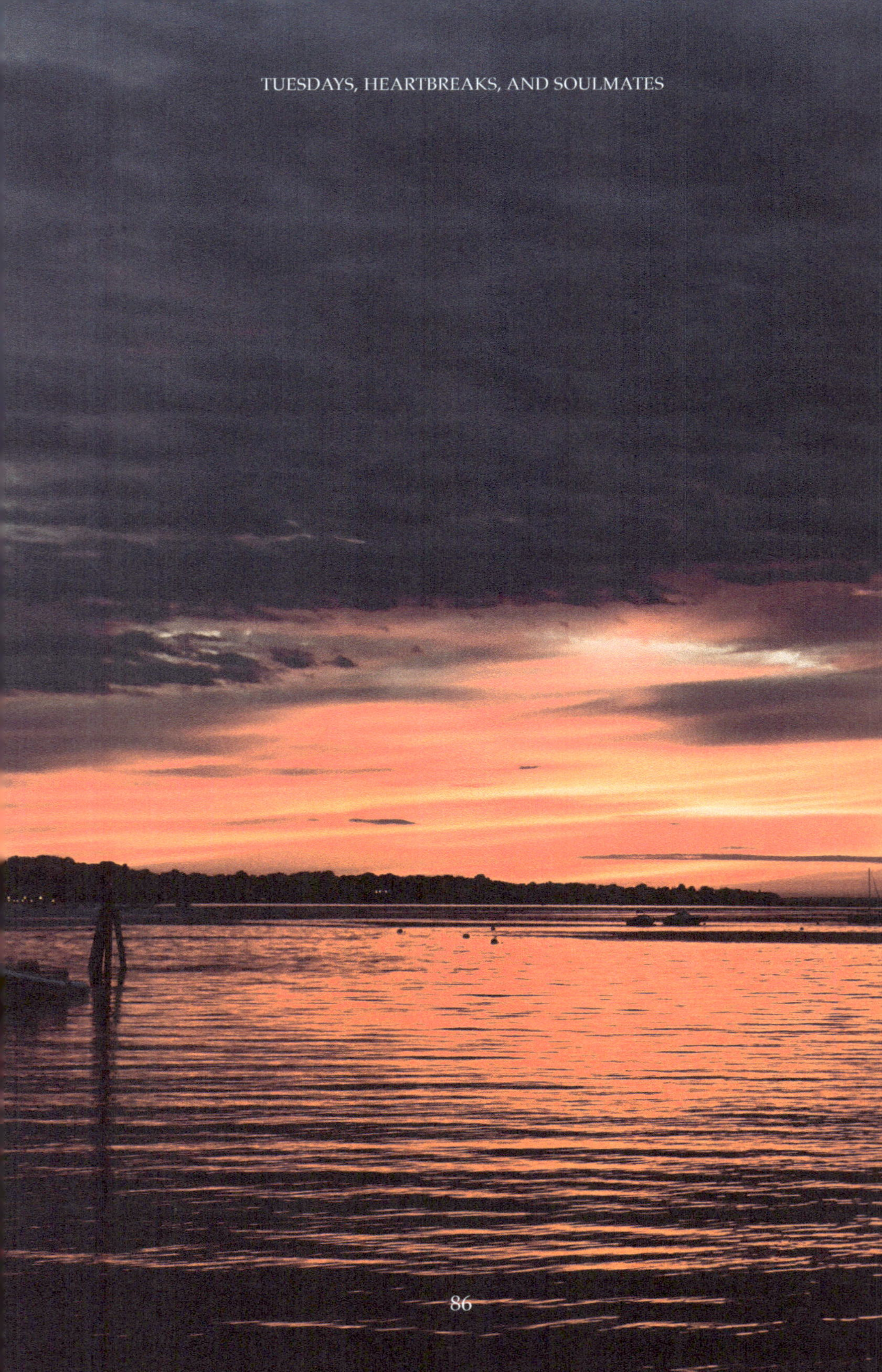

She attempted to fight

the pirates that wanted to steal

what was in her heart

Battles of tortured soul

heartbroken, nearly defeated

the Port Jeff ferry arrived

just in the nick of time

to save her from

the *storm* inside her head

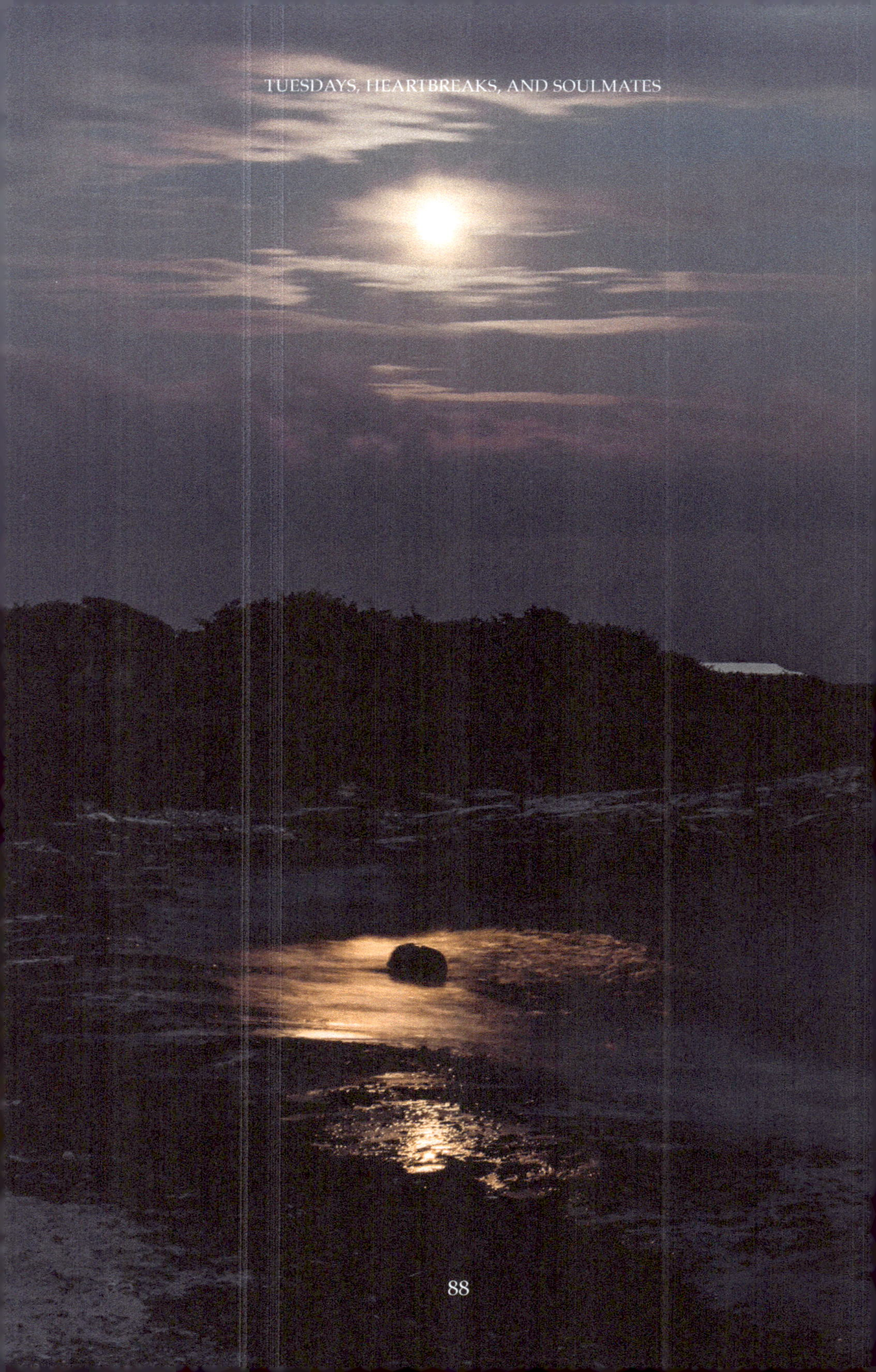

Eyes the color of celestite

Hidden treasures of a cosmic *lullaby*

There is hope in this story

I have been here for all of your life

and you will be here for all of mine

everlasting love through every season

because that is the bones we are made of

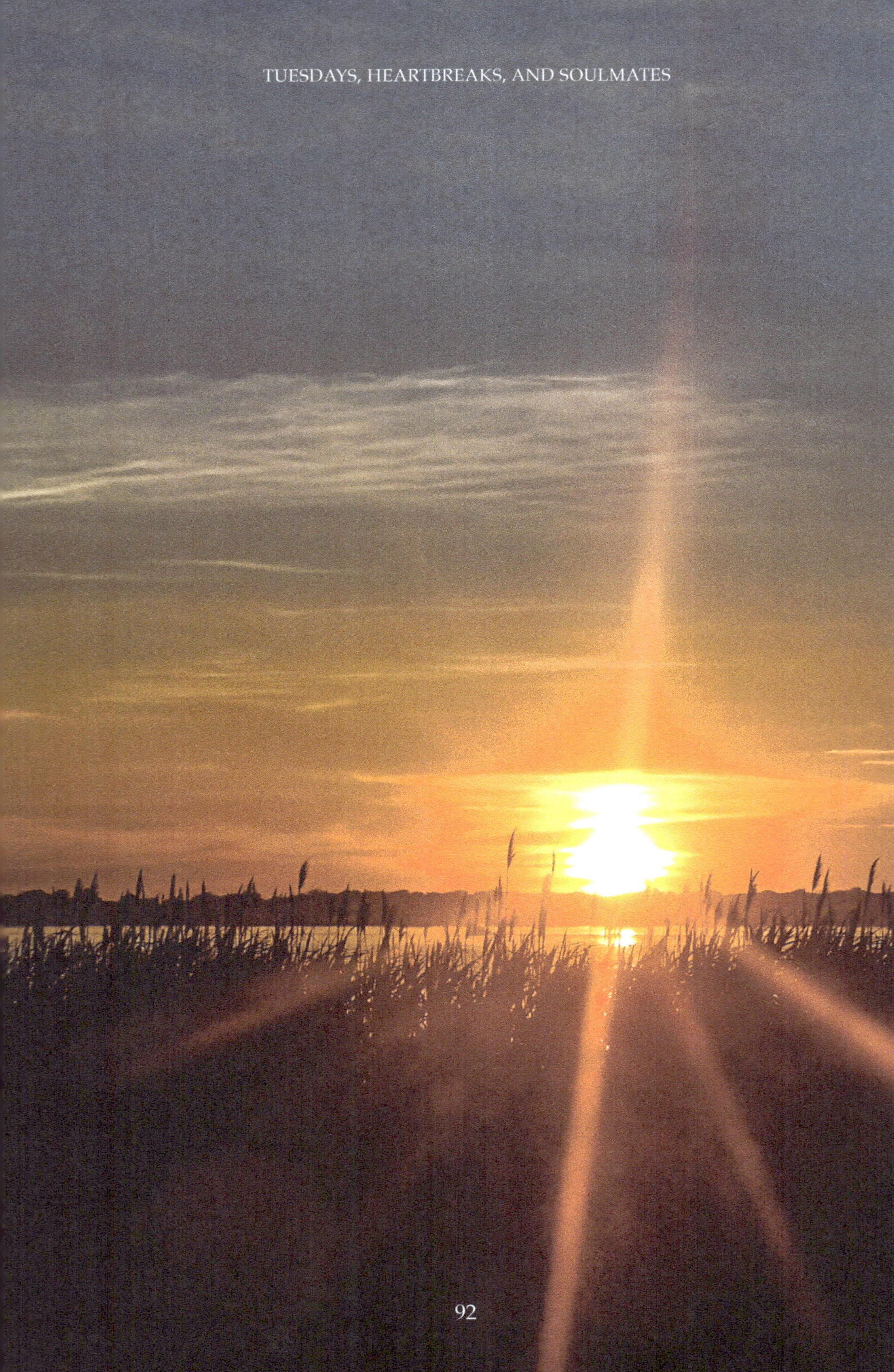

I carry around fragments of memories

from experiences that taught me

Unconditional love, patience, and depth

the *alchemy* of us

the pursuit of a grand adventure

and a picturesque transformation of life

There she is, overflowing with joy
Her most cherished version of self yet
Living in harmony, Without Fear
Adventure. Self-expression. Art. Love. Music.
Emotional depth. Poetry. Fairy godmother.
Conscious connection between soulmates
crashing our hearts, lifetime after lifetime
showing up as the most authentic self
knowing beyond a shadow of doubt
She is love—the kind that brings *you* back home

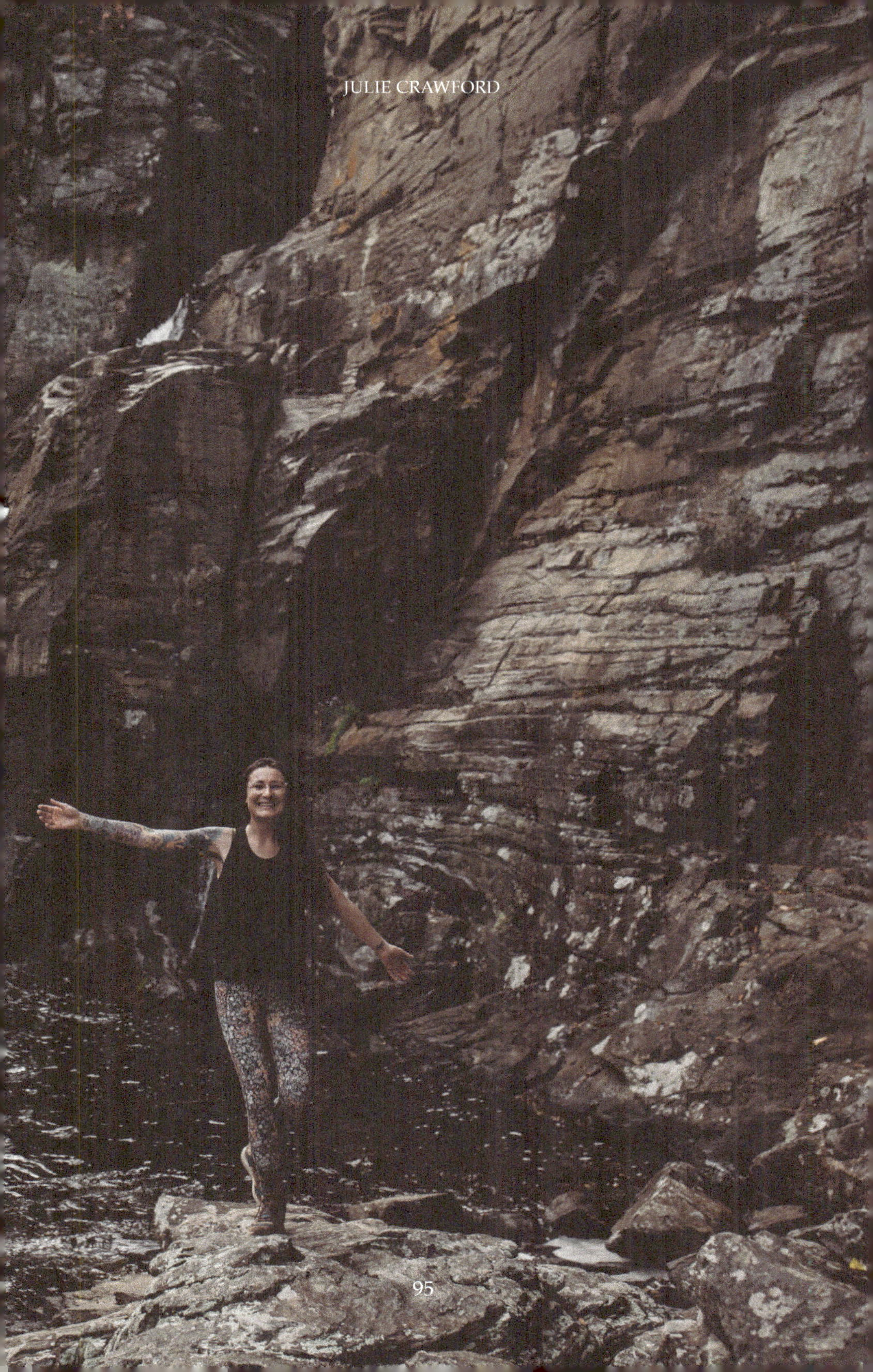

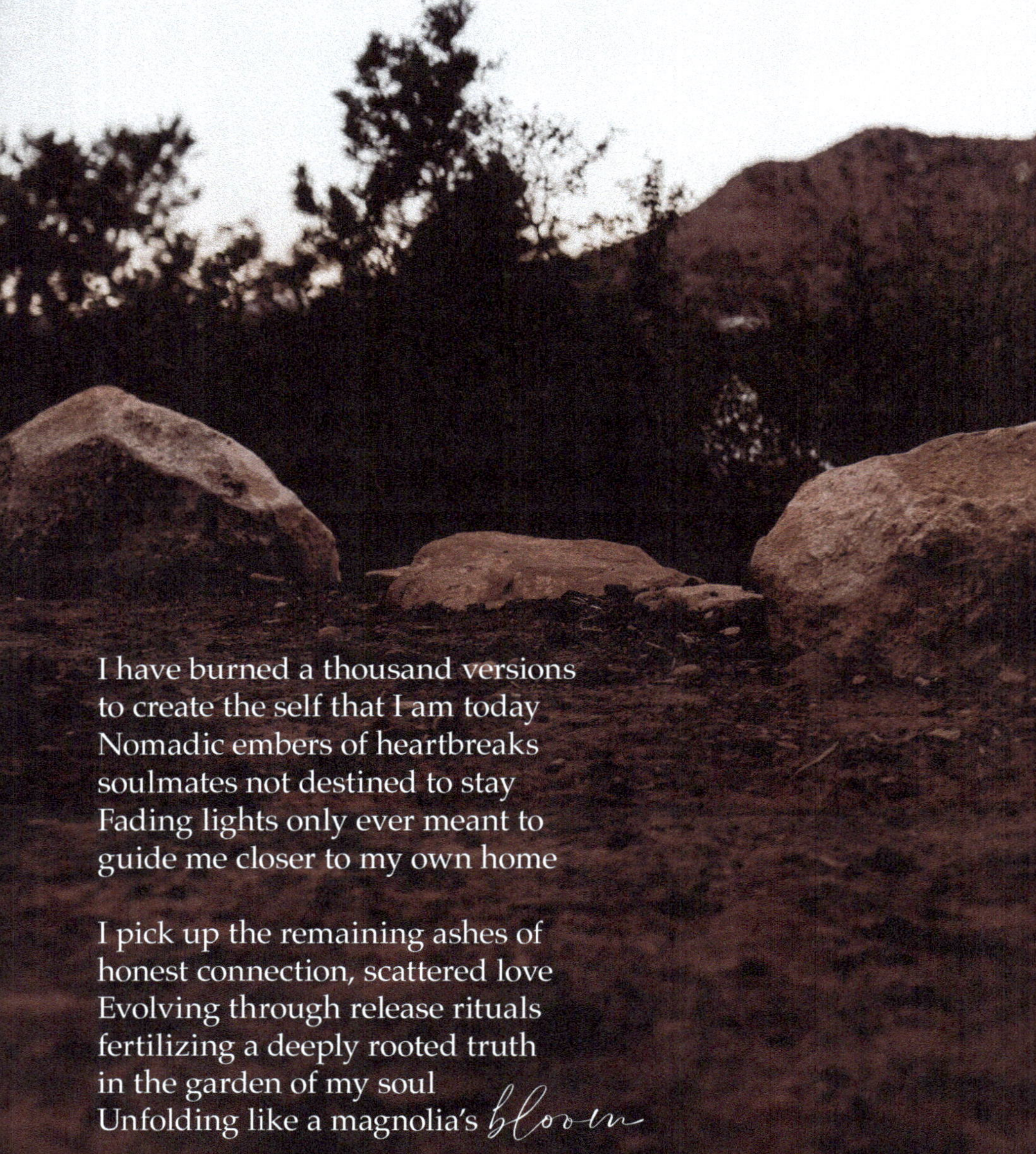

I have burned a thousand versions
to create the self that I am today
Nomadic embers of heartbreaks
soulmates not destined to stay
Fading lights only ever meant to
guide me closer to my own home

I pick up the remaining ashes of
honest connection, scattered love
Evolving through release rituals
fertilizing a deeply rooted truth
in the garden of my soul
Unfolding like a magnolia's *bloom*

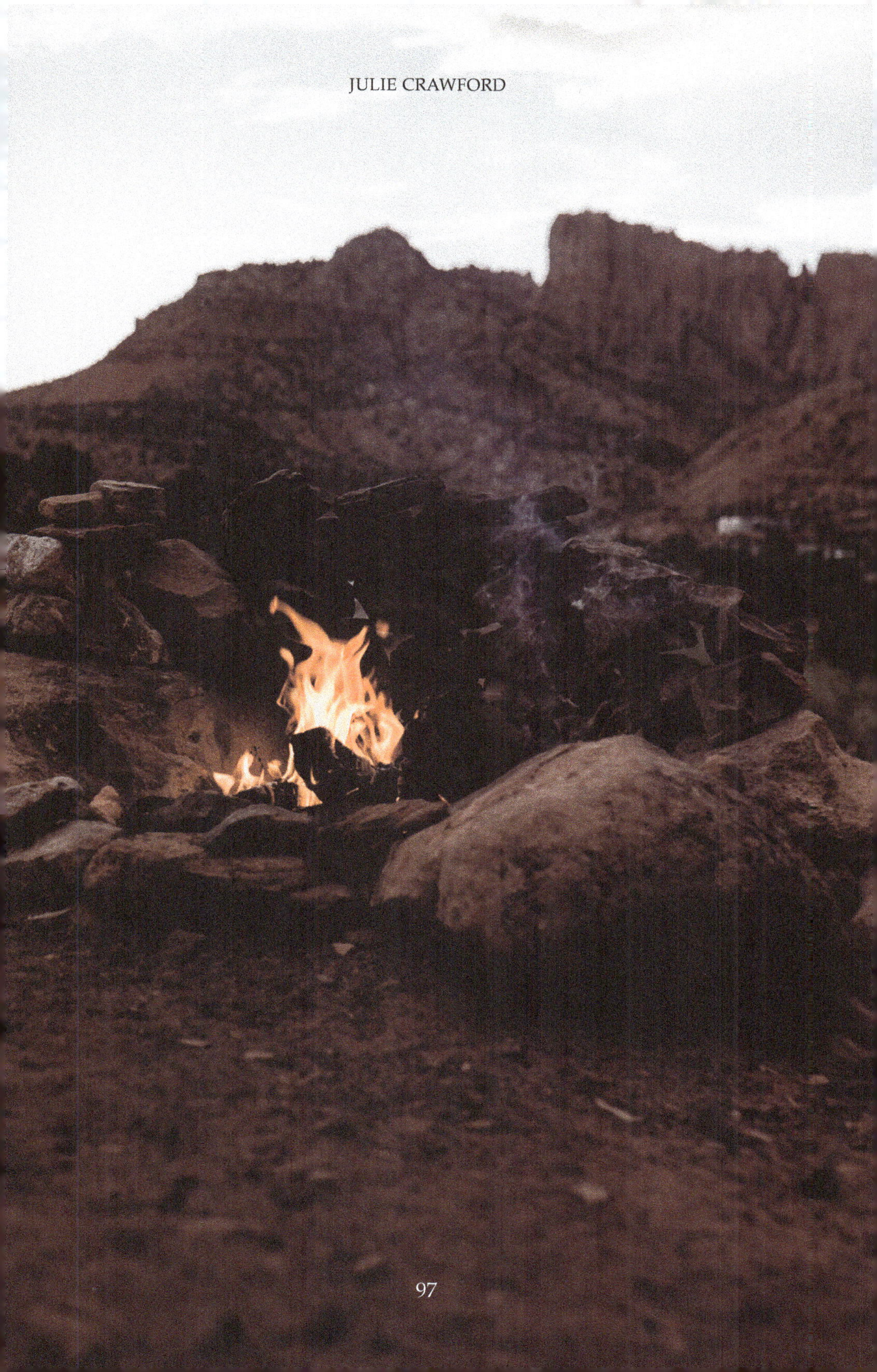

What if the asterisks

in *you* were a sign

of the *daisies*

Symbolizing purity

True love nectar

New beginnings

Motherhood

My birth flower

Foretelling of home life

What if the *you* was *me*

Destined to be found

Molded into the woman

I dreamed of becoming

Heart on my shoulder

Guardian *angel*

Caring for loved ones

Seeing in myself

My mother

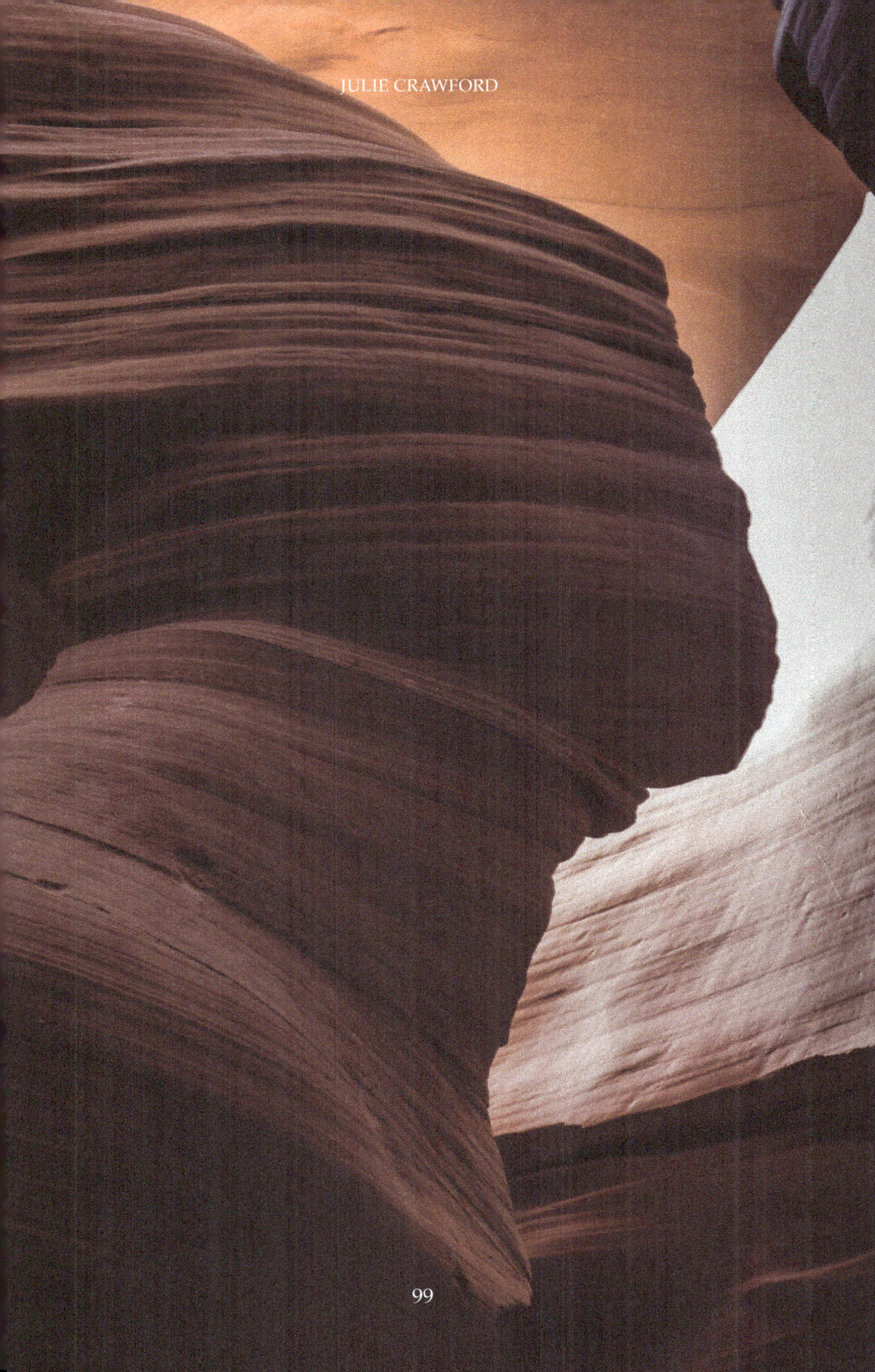
JULIE CRAWFORD

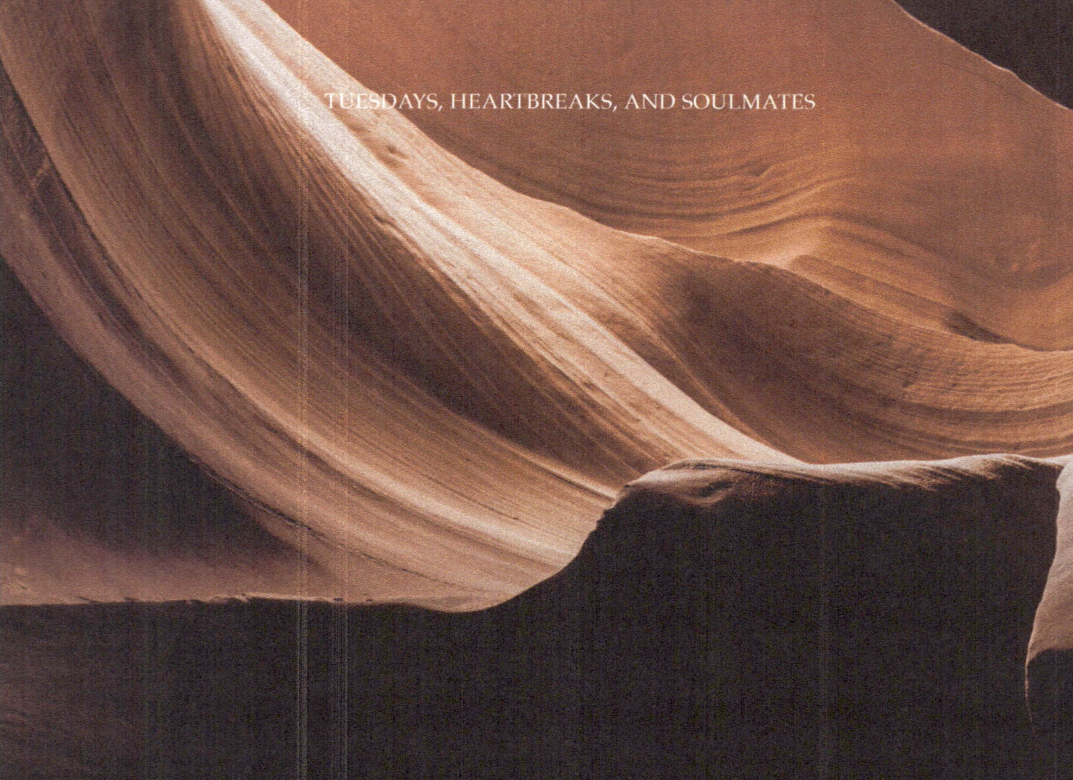

11 years ago, it was a hurt in my babies that reflected my own
Grasping the fact that I am to blame is excruciatingly painful

Family, love, and a sense of home are deeply rooted in my life
Courses I let consume me were shots in the dark to find the same

I thought your energy could only be found in another person
Never in all these years realizing I had power instilled in me
to manifest the entirety of my searches within my own self

You have built an empire, chief of the tribe, a protective force
yet patient and kind, a calm through any storm inside and out

Now, I am able to see pieces of you reflecting in my own image
and being able to show up for family is my greatest achievement

Your fatherly love, leadership, and mindset is a *gift* to all

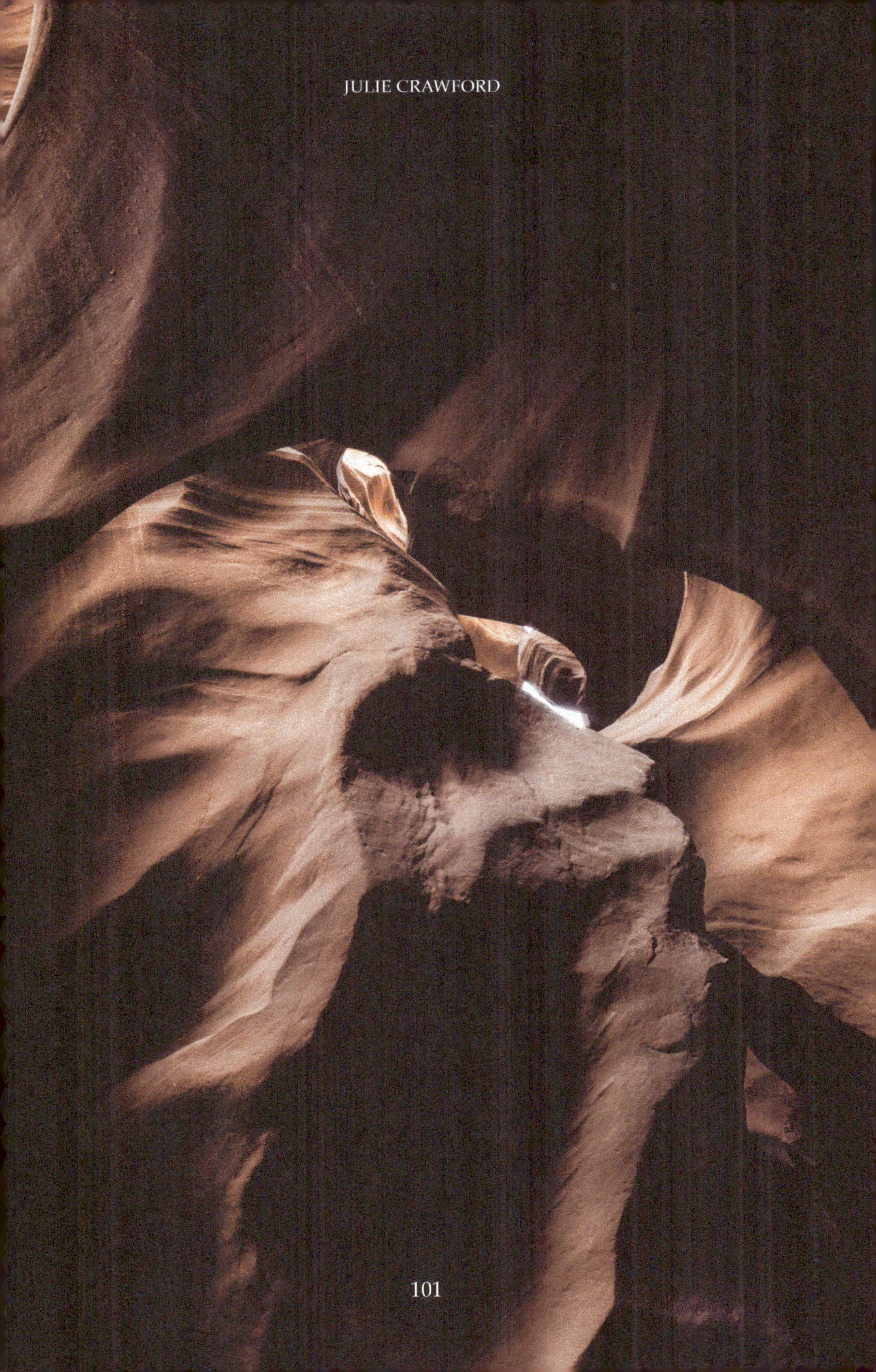

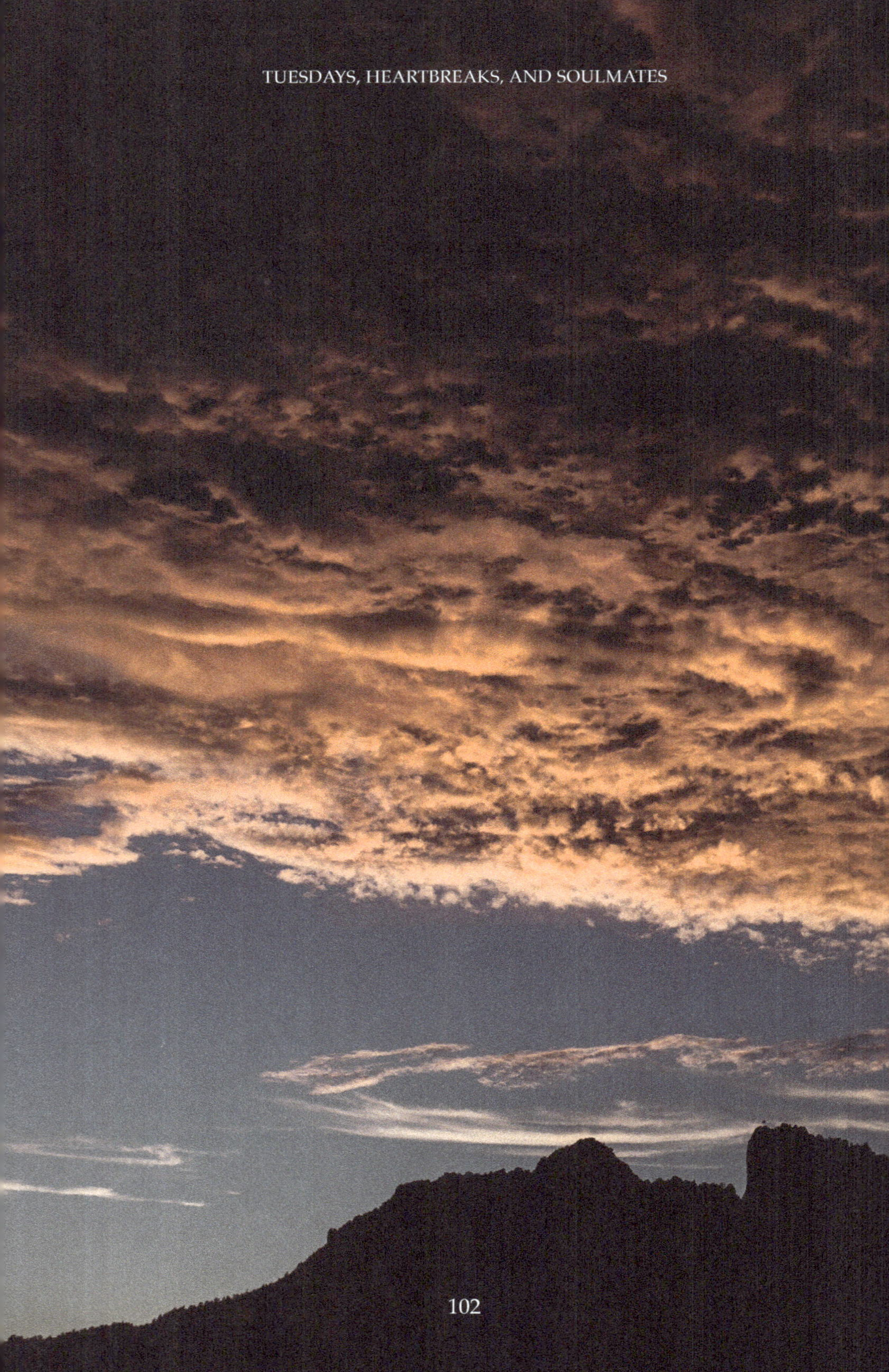

Give the world your song

your *kaleidoscopic* aura

Find the courage to speak your truth

Be kind to yourself, never vilify your past

Support your growth, seek expansion

and vastly show up in this space

that is meant to be yours

We come across people in life
placed in our path through
what I can only describe as
divinely orchestrated timing
These gentle *(sometimes not)* souls
hold keys to pieces of our truth
locked away in the subconscious
Through human connection
and a sprinkle of metaphysics
we are given the opportunity to
see the self-reflection and the
chance to choose to grow within

Soulmates *(and heartbreaks)*

Sometimes we meet people in life
and feel an instant soul recognition
beyond reasonable explanation

We collide with these kindred spirits
taking us to the next level within
affirmation we are on the right path

Sometimes these precious soulmates
regardless of how much deep the connection
cannot choose to stay for the long journey

You have to get down to the *heart* of the matter
learn to live without them and let soft memories
cultivated in honest love flow through your soul

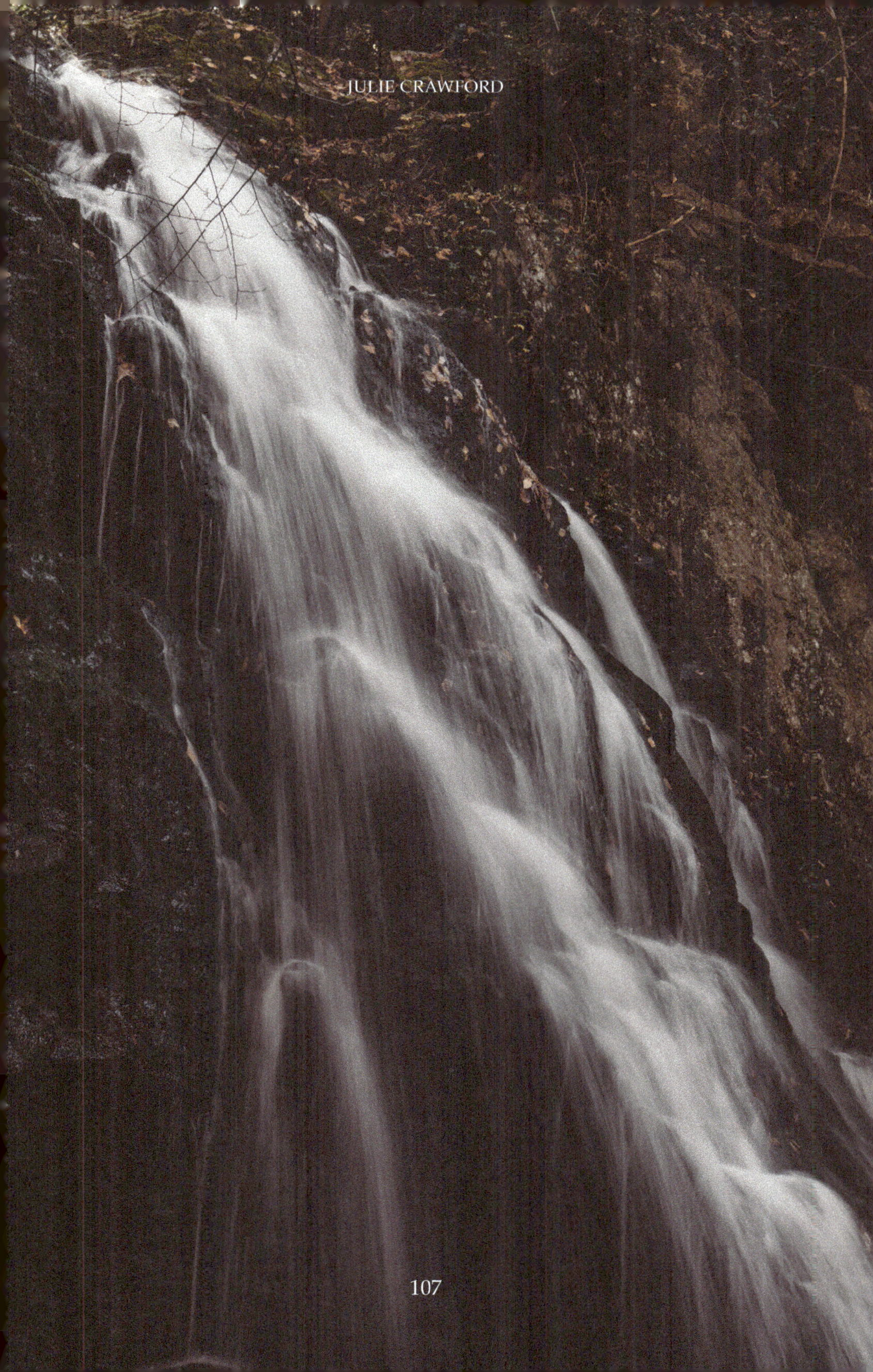
JULIE CRAWFORD

once upon a time

There was a field trip
in the mountains
Lessons about
reptiles and amphibians
and their habitats
How to forge reverie
in the blacksmith shop
How to read paper maps
carve affection
in fallen branches
Mastering sustainability
Blossoming vulnerability
like the pine cones need fire
and I thirst for your water
Learning adventure
and how to fall in love

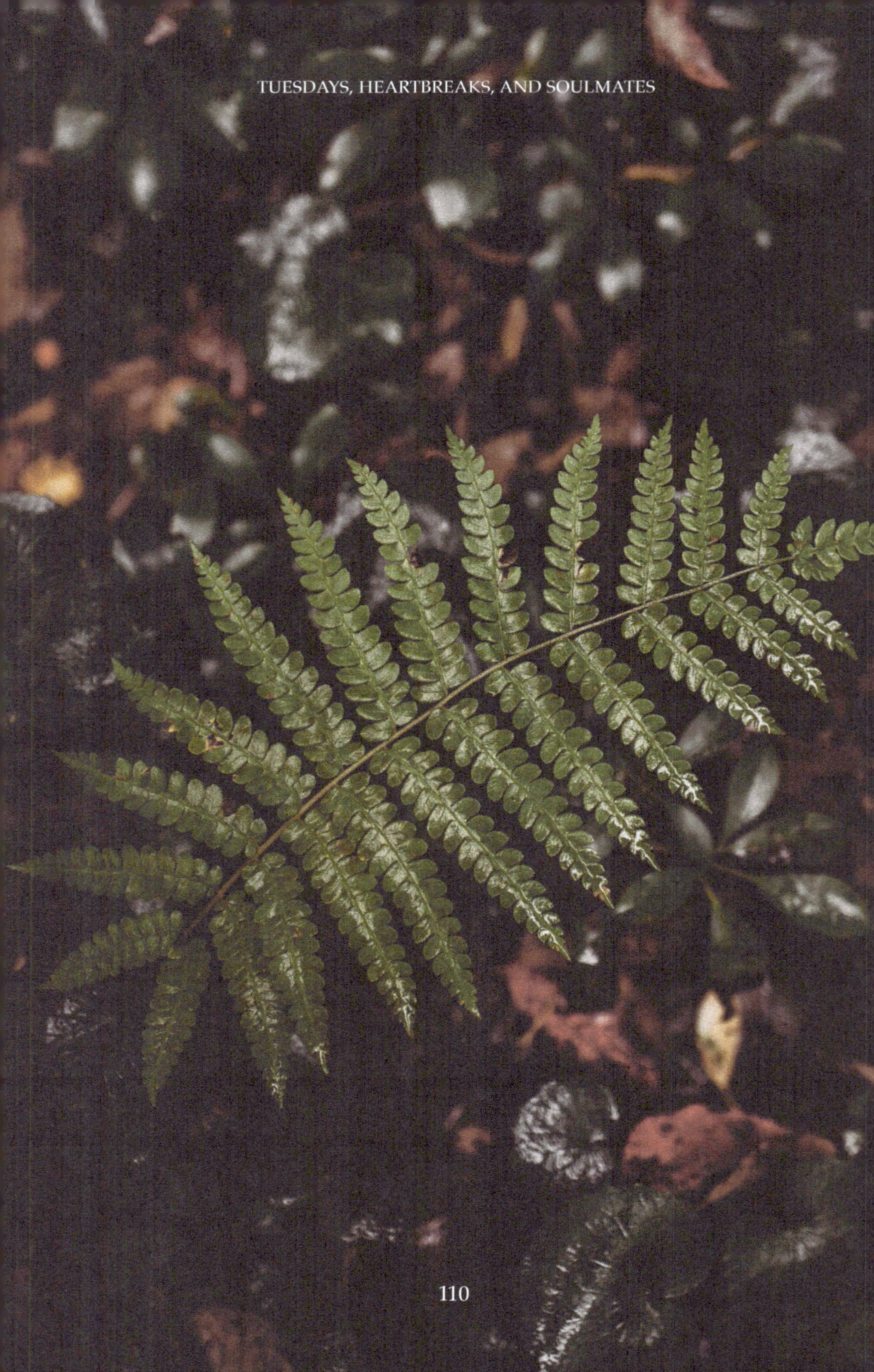

To *my person,*

I trust you will arrive when this journey is
meant to be shared together in this lifetime
When we both evolve to the individuals
with the capacity to hold a love so grand
Every path I pursue carries the prayer
of manifesting our divine connection
I look for you everywhere and
no matter the route, I cannot find you
Understanding the beauty of Tuesdays
painful heartbreaks and shadow work
and loving moments with dearest soulmates
I have come to realize that all I should ever be
chasing is myself and to keep moving forward
I feel the essence of invincible connection
harmony and tenderness in the sincerity
I will continue to pour my heart into
soulful passions and achieve my dreams
May you be doing the same in your world
I will follow all the synchronicity, the numbers,
the lyrics, the adventures, and every calling
because amidst it all is truth and where
I feel the abundance of life—homely ground
Home is where I will be waiting for you
May this book find you someday and
reading the words and seeing the photograph
allow you to recognize my love as your own
As I live this wildly intentional
and flourishing existence of mine
just being my loving self
I carry the faith that
you will find your way back to me

I feel you coming home, you are almost here

I am committed to choosing my most loving self

at every turn knowing my light is your map

Our souls are magnets, metaphysical gravity

We have been waiting patiently for connection

Surrendering to the process of unlearning and

learning our way to our favorite version of self

Because it is only there, *twin flames* collide

into one another and become inseparable

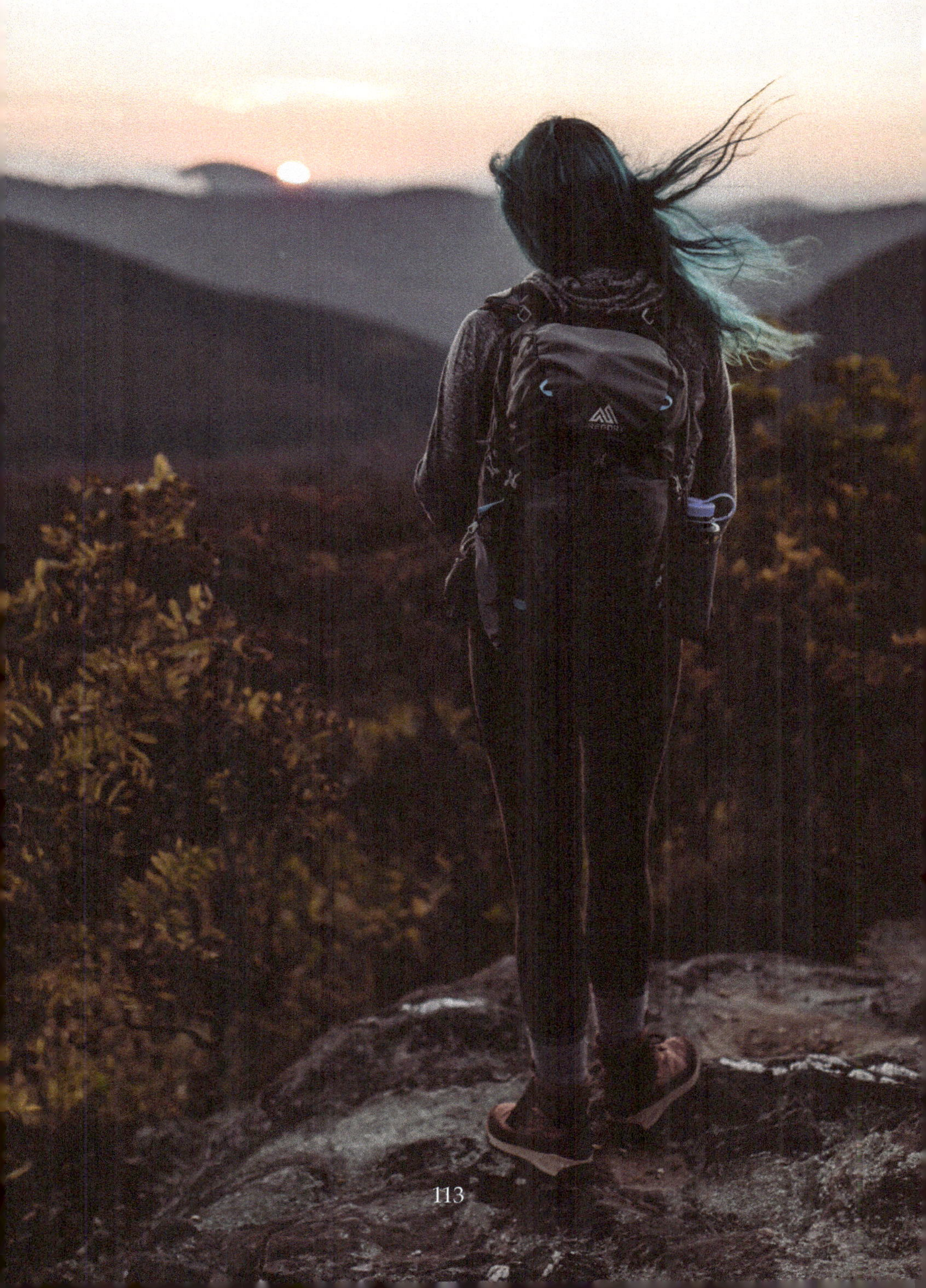

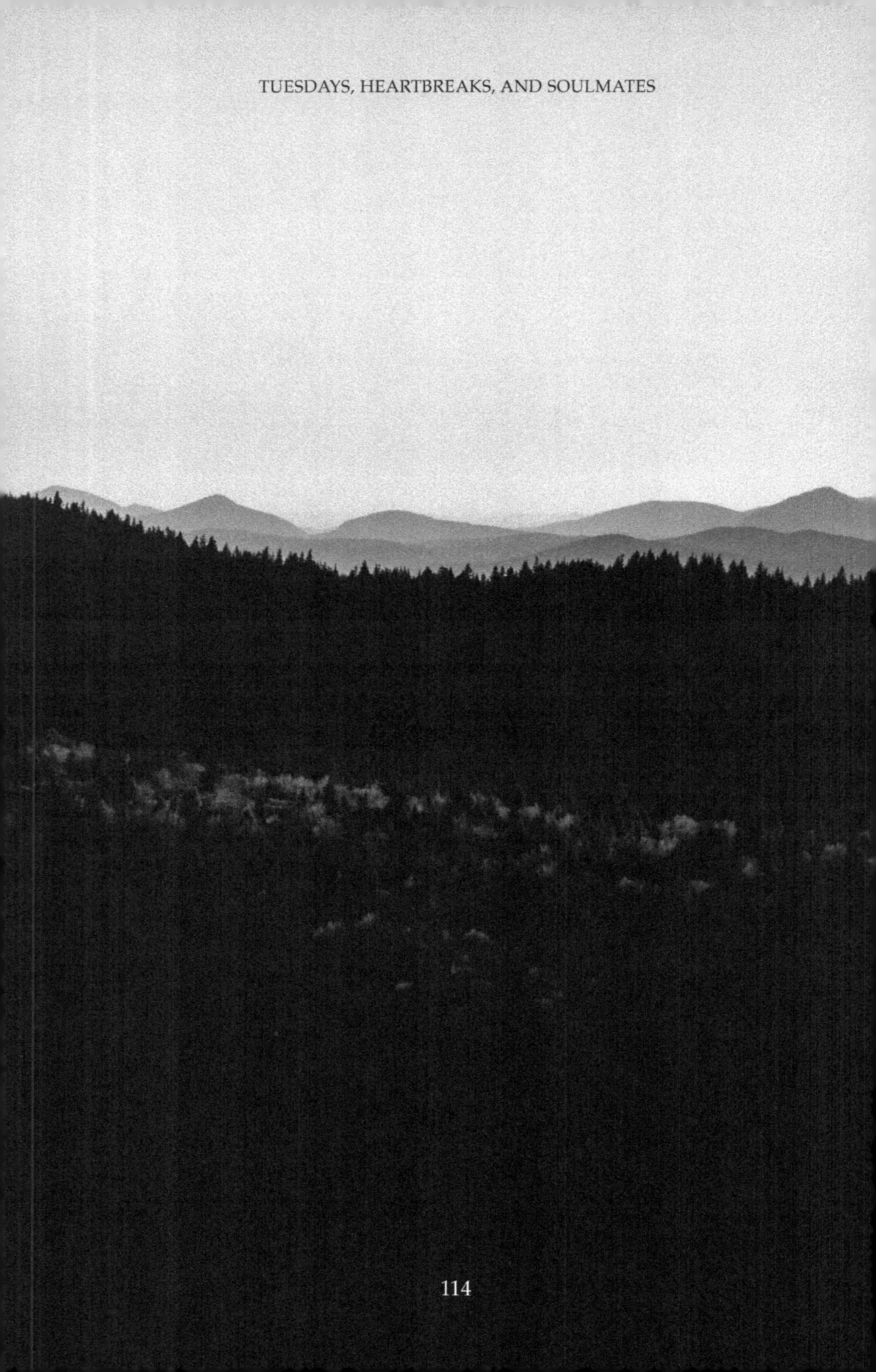

Every experience moves me closer

to the person I am meant to be

Every lesson guides my soul closer

to finding *unwavering* love

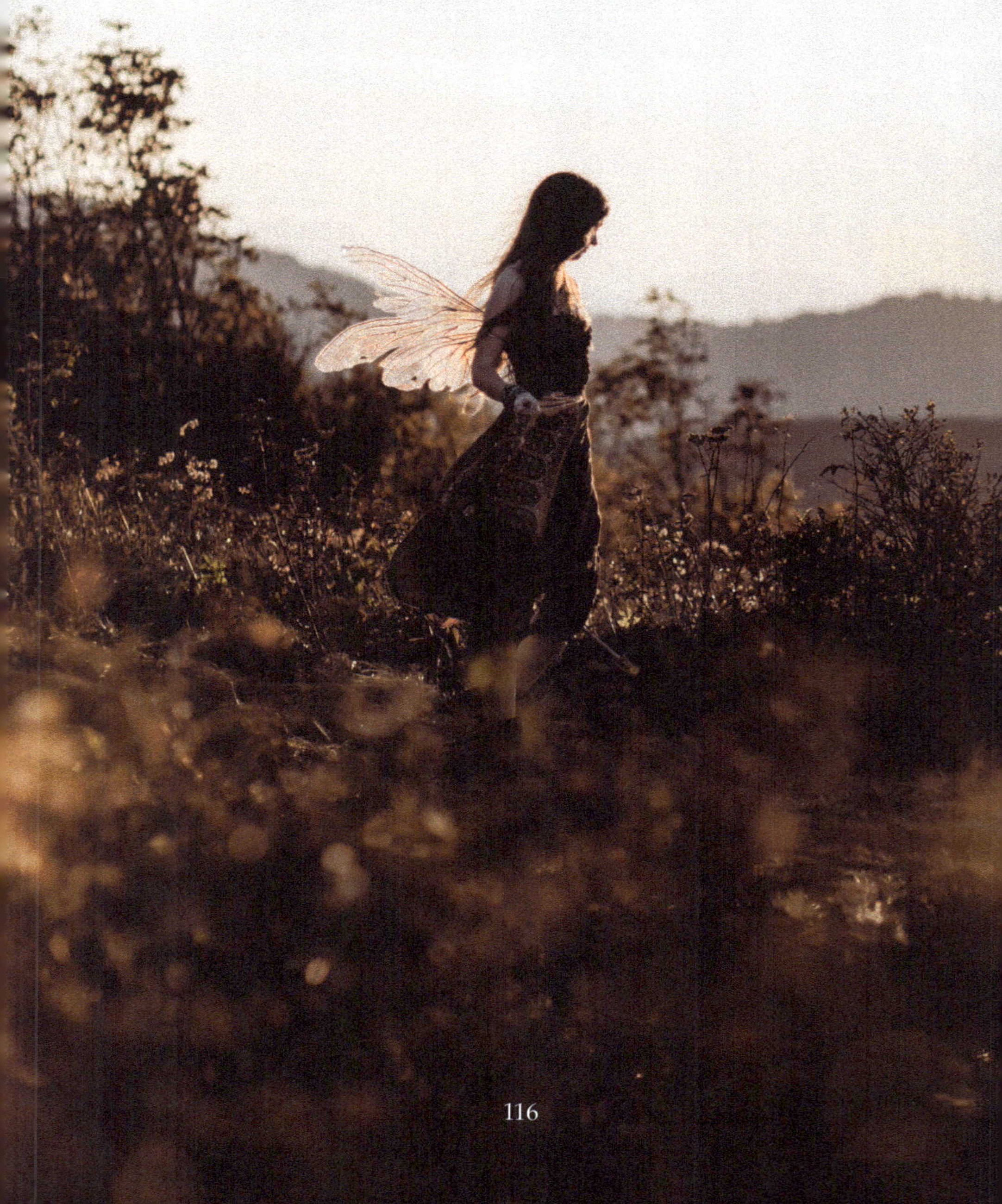

She is one with nature

Dancing among golden *wildflowers*

as they sway to the same rhythm

Singing a gentle hymn to the *mountains*

as winds carry her notes as their own

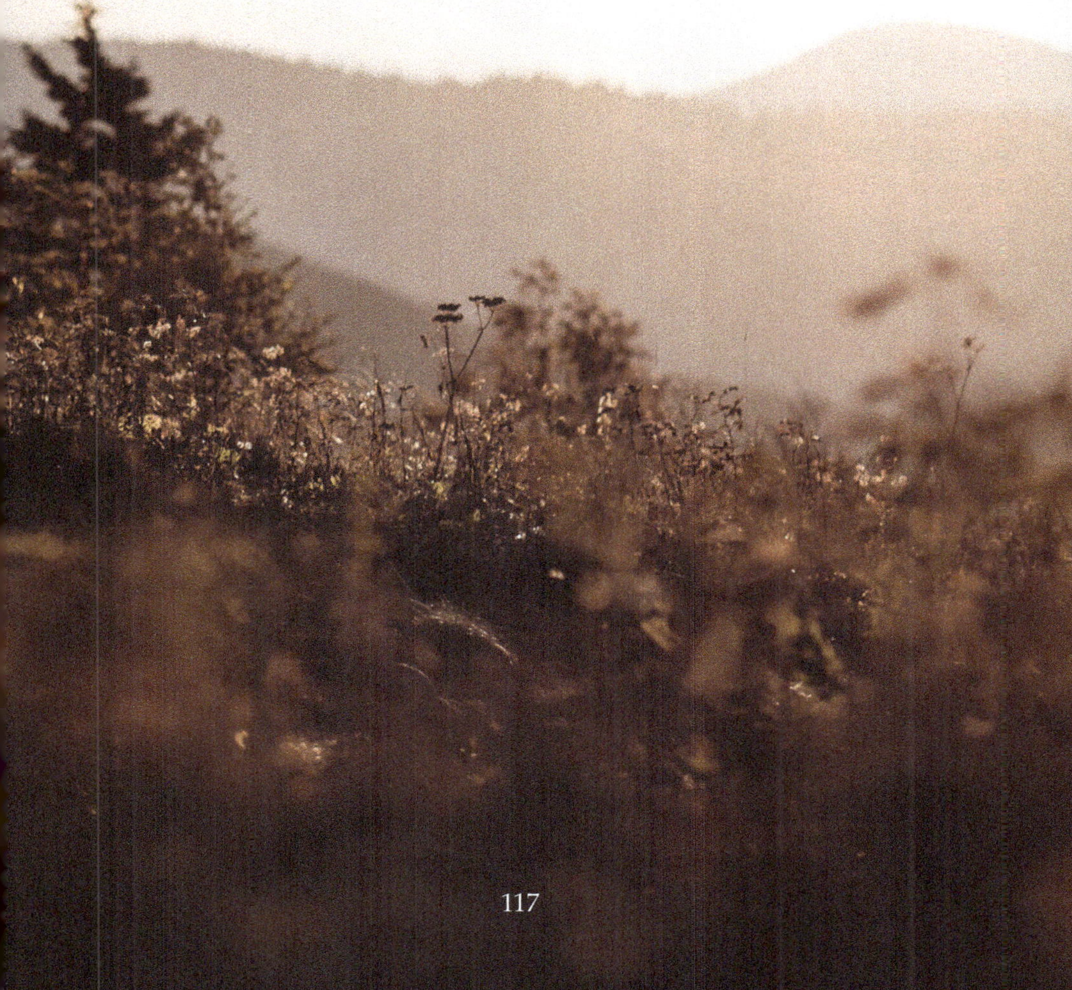

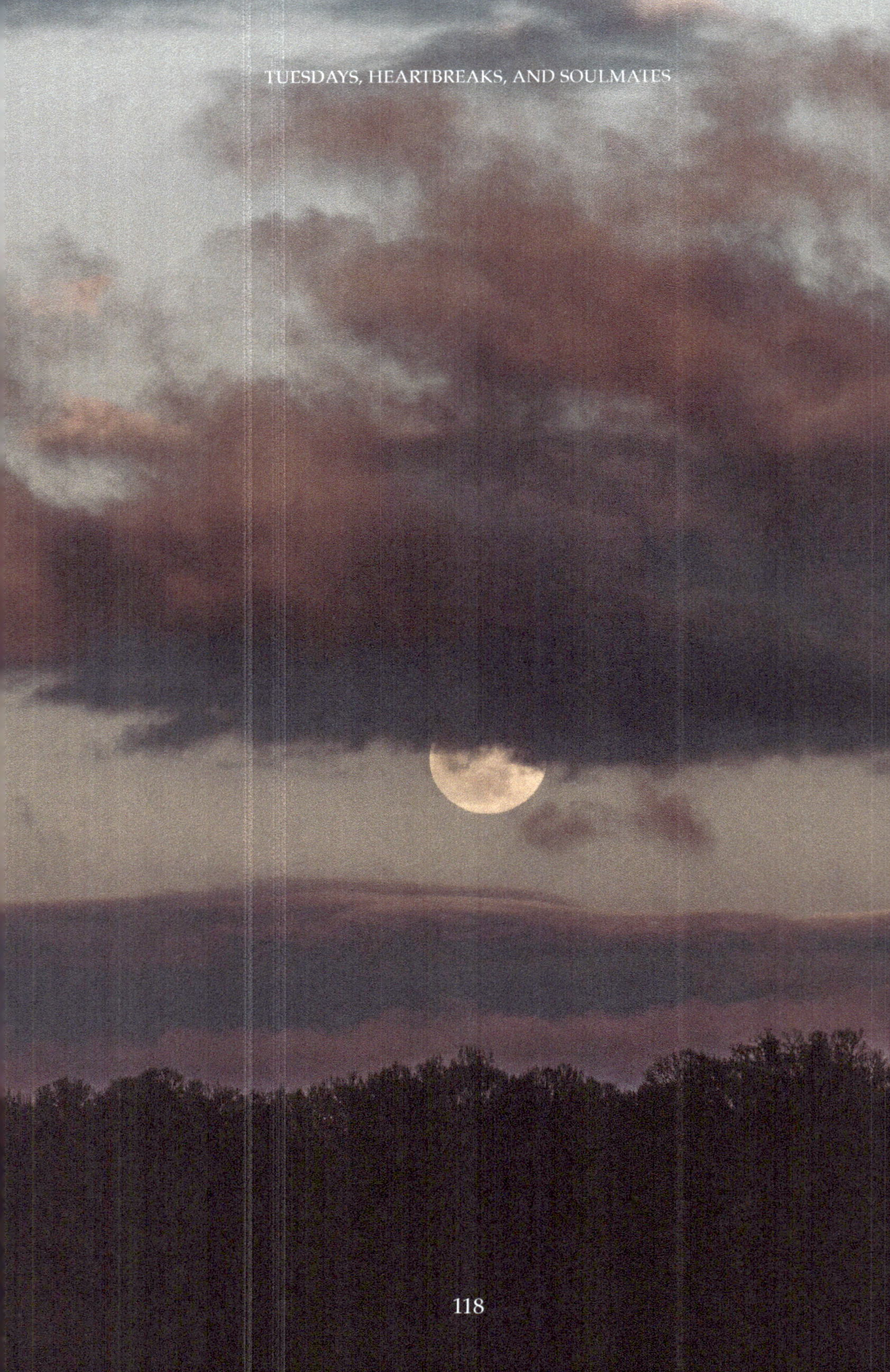

Before the *entwining*
of soulmates
could ever come into
conscious awareness
I had to follow my truth
rather than any falsities
set in place by others
even by my own limits
It was a tough journey
to where I now stand
but worth every effort
I have intentionally
shed layers upon layers
destroying the walls
I built to shelter myself
from painful rejection
Looking back at phases
understanding that
self-imposed barriers
are mostly to blame
Ultimate heartbreak
I never exposed my
vulnerable side thus
never giving myself
a chance to truly be *loved*

No matter how tightly I held on
the ending was always inevitable
I would have to say goodbye

Hand-drawn *colors* on my wrist
to keep your essence close to me
even the permanent ink faded *(twice)*

Maybe there is an alternate universe
we are floating the river of life together
but here, I must learn to let go of October

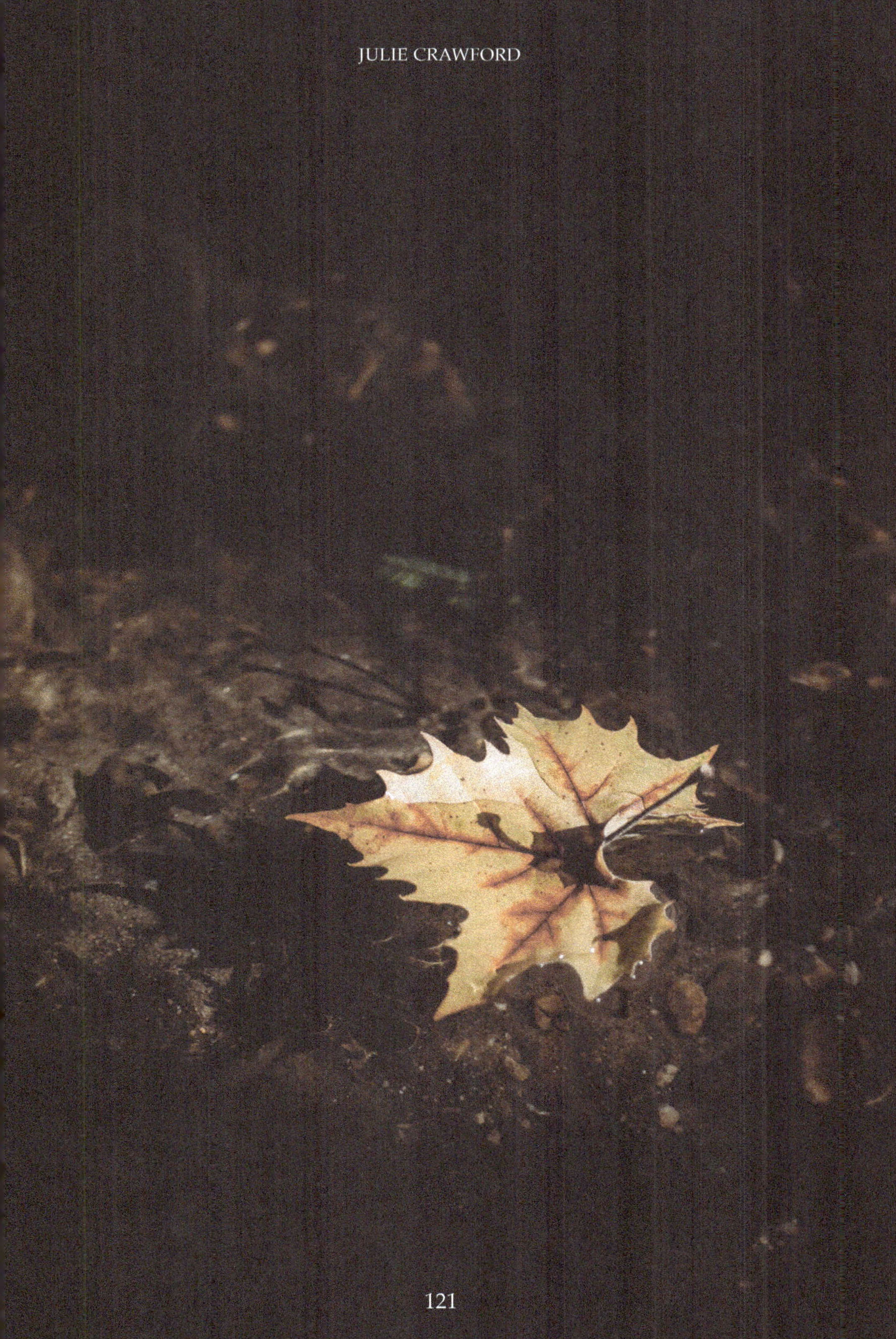

You are energetic euphoria

Familiarity of a *past life* connection

Meant to love me back home

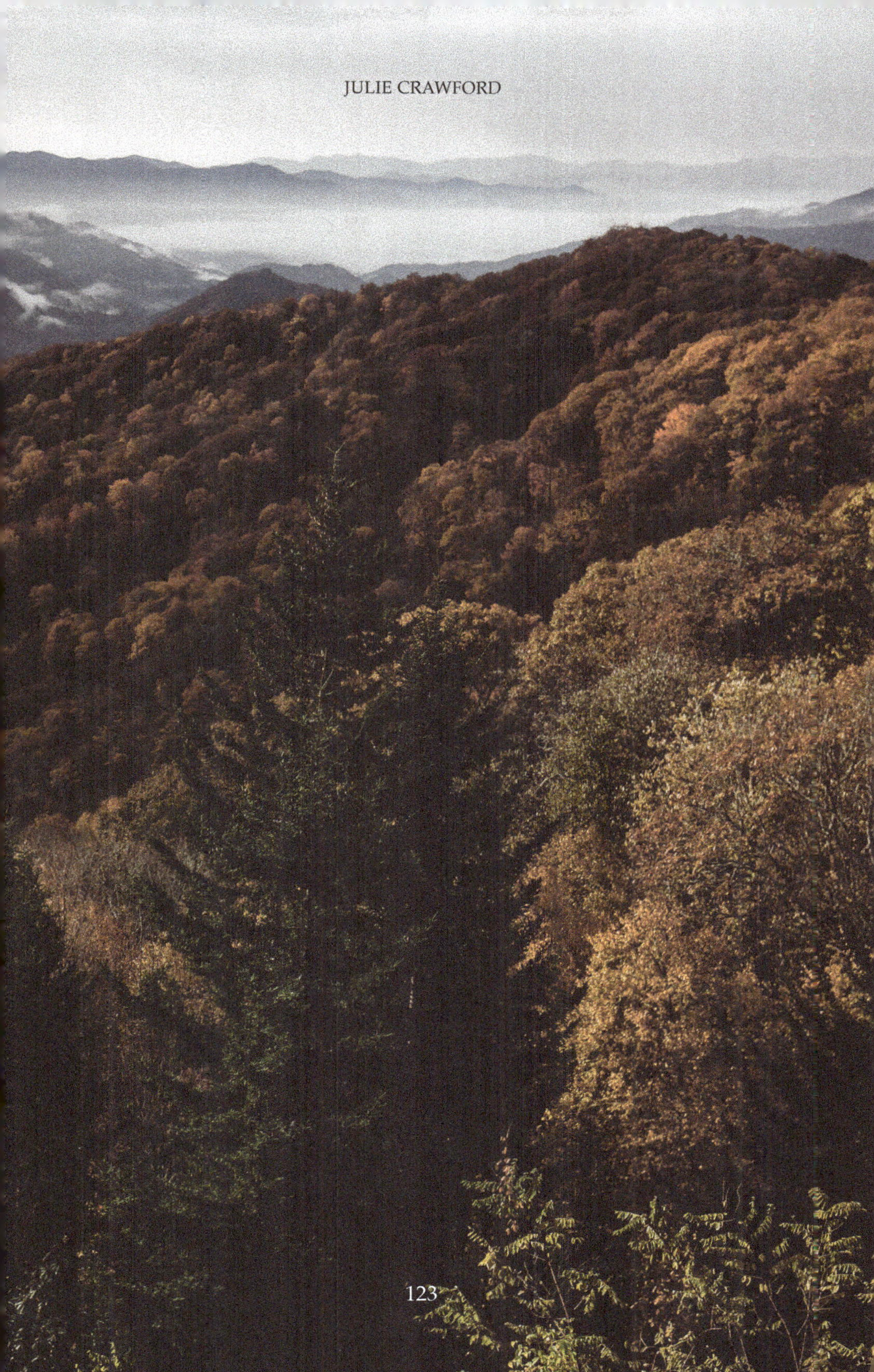

Dear November,

You've been my *favorite* for a while

The power held within your days

The pieces of me that only you've found

The crisp smell of change that awaits

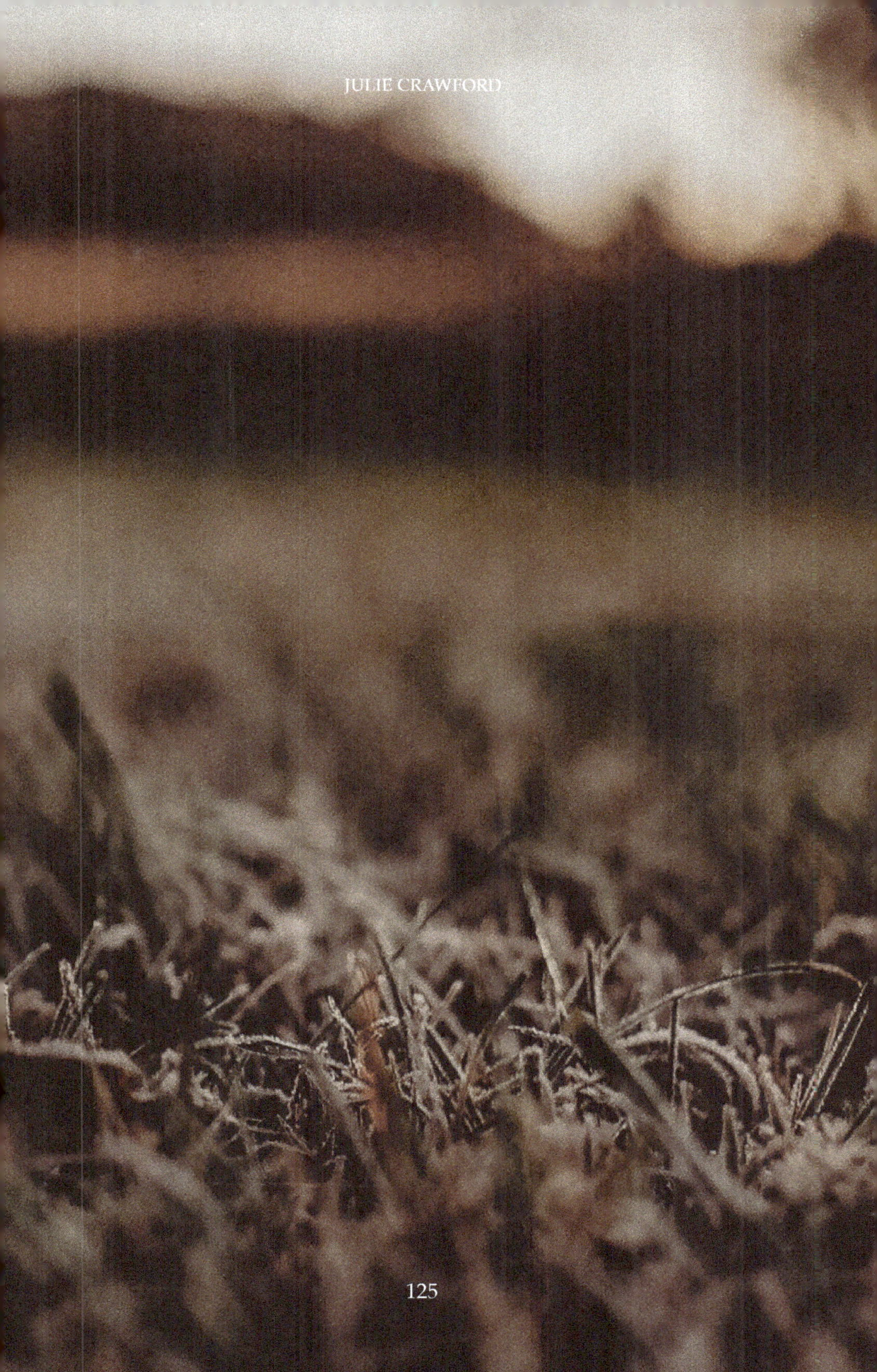

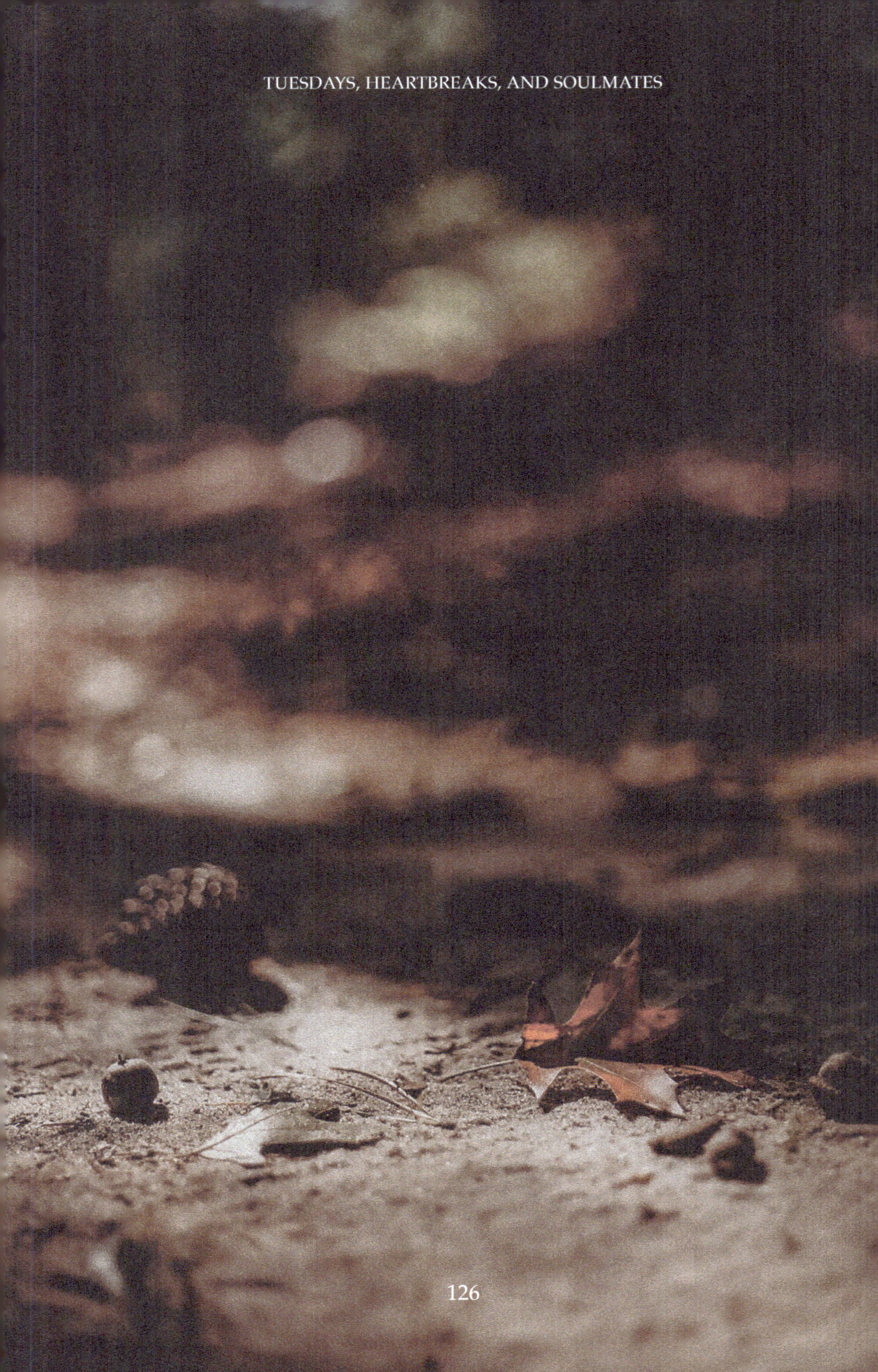

When the moon is full

and that song starts to play

forget me not

in thoughts of the mountains

our hikes and that waterfall

in the colors of autumn leaves

and the taste of cider on your lips

When the *winter* comes

and the snow begins to fall

may *evergreen* memories

hold and keep you warm

and remind you of honest love

The love that you seek

is the *love* that has lived

Within you all along

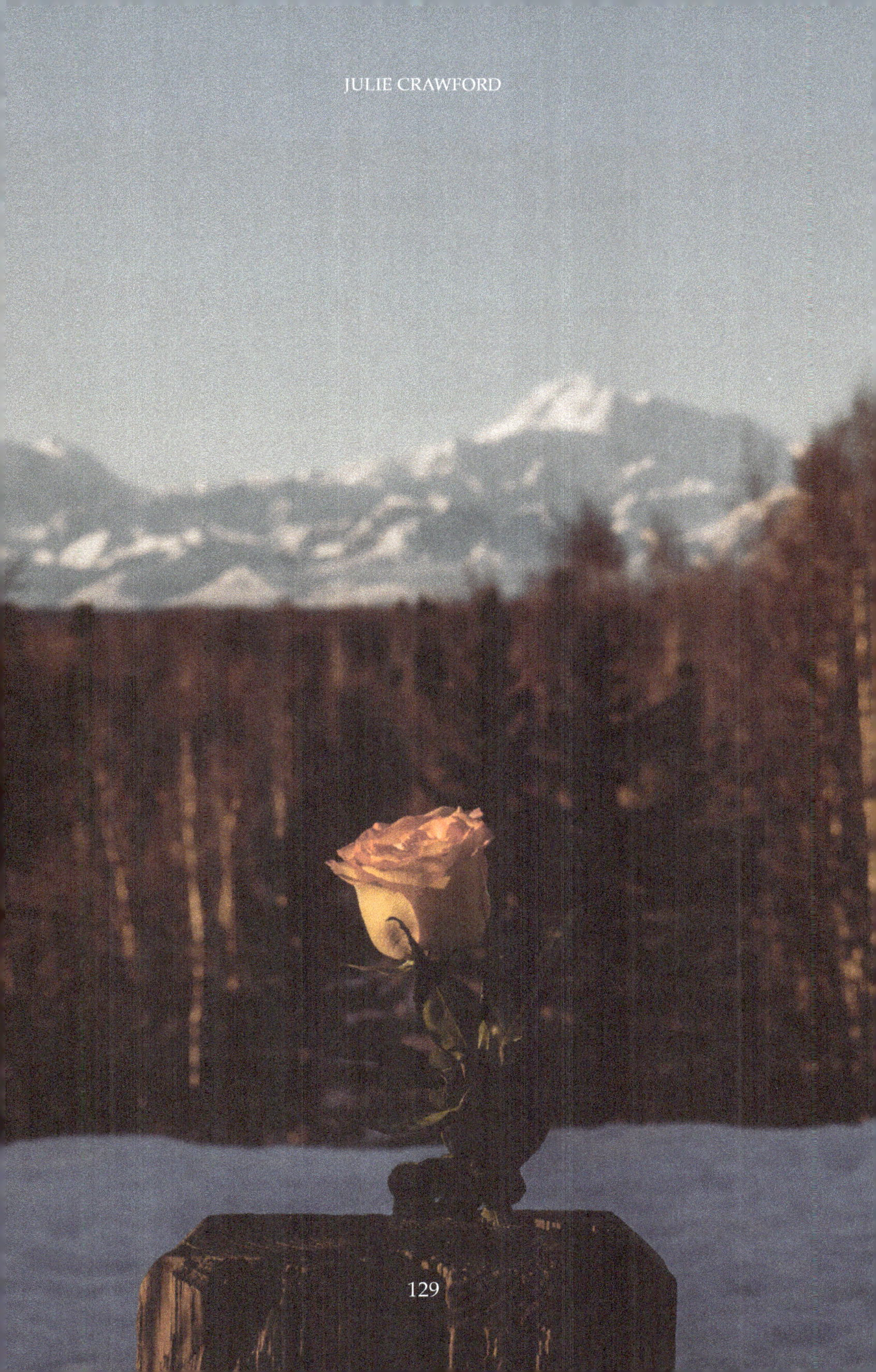

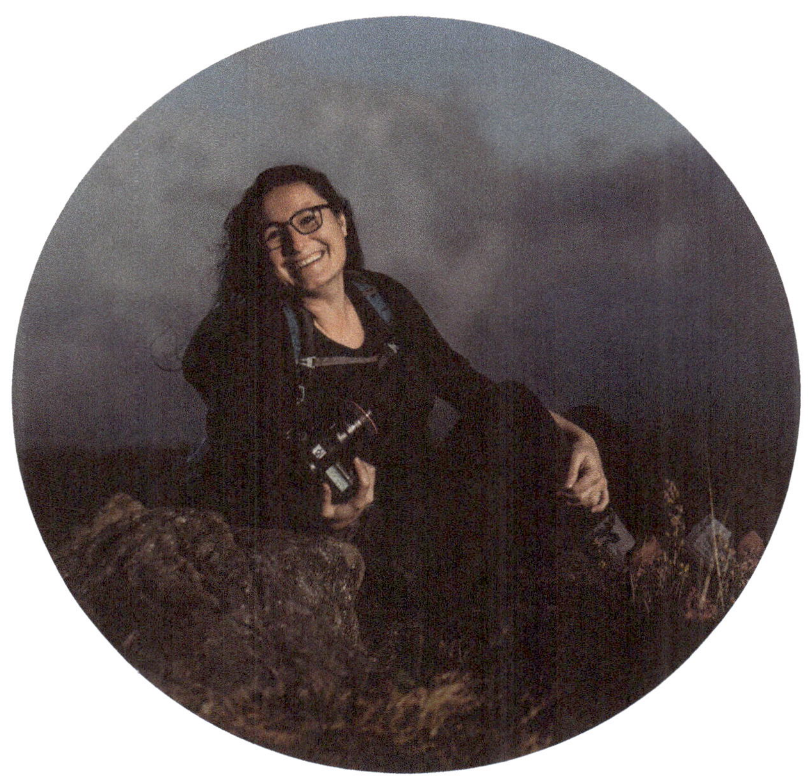

Julie Crawford is a passionate creator of wildly intentional experiences throughout her professional career and personal life. Along with storytelling of her journey through the path of self-discovery, she travels around the world planning and photographing adventure elopements with couples who share the same appreciation for wanderlove experiences. All she gains from experiences, the personal growth and emotional connection, fuels the creative energy that goes into crafting elopements amidst the wild—her artistry known as Magnolia and Ember.

photo by Rachel Clift
rcliftpoetry.com
@r.cliftpoetry

Magnolia + Ember
magnoliaandember.com
@magnoliaandember

@CAMP_CRAWFORD